The
VEGETABLE
Bible

The
VEGETABLE
Bible

A comprehensive guide to
growing, preserving,
storing, and cooking
your favorite
vegetables

Tricia Swanton

THUNDER BAY
P·R·E·S·S
San Diego, California

Thunder Bay Press

An imprint of Printers Row Publishing Group
10350 Barnes Canyon Road, Suite 100, San Diego, CA 92121
www.thunderbaybooks.com

Printers Row Publishing Group is a division of Readerlink Distribution Services, LLC.
The Thunder Bay Press name and logo are trademarks of
Readerlink Distribution Services, LLC.
All correspondence concerning the content of this book should be addressed to
Thunder Bay Press, Editorial Department, at the above address.

Thunder Bay Press

Publisher:	Peter Norton
Publishing Team:	Lori Asbury, Ana Parker, Laura Vignale
Editorial Team:	JoAnn Padgett, Melinda Allman, Traci Douglas
Production Team:	Blake Mitchum, Rusty von Dyl

Interior layout and design by
Moseley Road Inc, www.moseleyroad.com

President:	Sean Moore
General Manager:	Karen Prince
Design Styling:	Philippa Baile
Design & Editorial:	Tina Vaughan
Layout:	Andy Crisp, Kate Stretton
Picture Research:	Jo Walton
Index:	Dan Connolly
Production Director:	Adam Moore

Library of Congress Cataloging-in-Publication Data

Swanton, Tricia.
The vegetable bible / Tricia Swanton.
    pages cm
ISBN 978-1-62686-436-8 (hardback)
1. Vegetable gardening. 2. Cooking (Vegetables) I. Title.
SB320.9.S93 2015
635--dc23
                    2015017393

Printed in China

19 18 17 16 15 1 2 3 4 5

CONTENTS

CONTENTS

INTRODUCTION: PRESERVING VEGETABLES

Vegetables are best eaten when fresh, in season, and preferably locally sourced—better for us, better for the environment, and better still if you grow your own vegetables. But what do you do when you find yourself with a bumper crop and a surplus of your favorite vegetable? Canning, drying, salting, and pickling are excellent ways to make full use of your bounty and extend the eating time and freshness of your vegetables throughout the year.

PICKLING, DRYING, AND SALTING

One of the simplest and easiest ways to preserve foods is to pickle them in acidic liquids, typically vinegar, lemon juice, or lactic acid, which inhibit the growth of bacteria. Pickles have a shelf life in the refrigerator of one month. Sun-drying is the oldest method for preserving foods; today this is done safely and easily in a food dehydrator or in a regular oven at a very low heat. The drying process removes moisture from the fresh vegetable and suppresses the growth of bacteria—this can also mean a loss of some vitamins, minerals, and other nutrients. Salting is an economical way to preserve vegetables while retaining most of their nutrients. Depending on the recipe, the salting process involves adding higher or lower levels of salt mixed with water or vinegar. Salting and drying are not for everyone, as the resulting foods have a salty taste and/or require soaking before eating.

Pickled cucumbers and sun-dried tomatoes

Salted kohlrabi

BENEFITS OF CANNING

Of all the methods for preserving vegetables, canning best retains the original flavor, texture, color, and versatility of the fresh vegetable. Canning vegetables offers a low-cost, healthy food source with an extended shelf life. When processed at their peak, canned vegetables retain their nutritional content. In some cases the beneficial properties of vegetables such as carrots, corn, pumpkins, and tomatoes are actively boosted by canning. Home-canned vegetables contain only what you decide to put into the jars; they are free from preservatives, stabilizers, and any other additives, and you are in full control over the salt and/or sugar content, if any. In addition the glass jars used in home canning contain none of the harmful chemicals associated with some commercially canned goods, the "packaging" is reused, and the whole process leaves a very small carbon footprint.

Vegetables harvested at their peak

Pickled and canned vegetables

CANNING AND FOOD SAFETY

The prime consideration in home canning is food safety.
Pressure canning is by far the safest method, and is the best
assurance against heat-resistant, potentially deadly botulism
(*Clostridium botulinum*), which can contaminate underprocessed
home-canned vegetables. Unlike fruits and tomatoes, which
are high-acid foods, vegetables are low-acid with a pH value
greater than 4.6. *Clostridium botulinum* loves a low-acid, low-
oxygen, moist environment, so in order to safely process canned
vegetables they must be pressurized to a temperature of 240°F.
Altitude is also a factor to consider when canning low-acid foods,
since water boils at lower temperatures in higher altitudes. In
addition, dial gauges must be checked for accuracy before each
canning session. In any case, whichever method you choose,
sterilized equipment in proper working order is a must. Before
canning at home, it is advisable to check the United States
Department of Agriculture's Complete Guide to Home Canning,
or visit the National Center for Food Preservation website.

FILLING THE JARS

Select young, tender vegetables as close as possible to
canning time. Wash and trim the vegetables and place them
into sterilized, preheated canning jars. You may parboil the
vegetables first or pack them raw. Cover the vegetables with
boiling water, leaving a 1-inch headspace between the top of the
liquid and the lid to allow for expansion—this is also necessary
to create a strong vacuum within the jar as it cools later on. (The
depth of headspace needed will vary according to the type of
vegetable, whether it is parboiled or raw, and your altitude level.)
You may add salt at this point for flavor, but it does not aid in the

Headspace between
vegetables and top of jar

Jars sterilized in boiling water
for 10 minutes

Place lid on jar,
add the screw
band, and tighten

preservation process. Canning salt will prevent the liquid from becoming cloudy. Using a spatula, remove air bubbles by gently moving the vegetables away from the sides of the jar. Place the lid on the jar, add the screw band, and tighten.

PRESSURE CANNING

Follow the manufacturers' instructions regarding how much water should be added to the pressure canner (typically 2–3 inches). Processing times vary according to the type of canner you are using, the vegetables being canned, and your altitude level. Heat the water in the canner and lower the cans into the pan. Close the lid tightly and keep on a high heat until steam is released from the vent pipe. Allow the air to continue to exhaust for ten minutes before placing the pressure regulator over the vent pipe. Once the gauge registers 11 pounds of pressure, set your timer. Maintain the required level of pressure for the recommended length of time. When this is done, turn off the heat and wait for the pressure to drop to zero. Use caution when opening the pressure canner so that trapped steam is released away from you. Remove jars and set aside to cool on a cooling rack or dish towel.

TESTING THE SEALS

As the jars cool, you should hear popping sounds as the vacuum inside the jar increases in pressure and the seals tighten. Once completely cold, test to see if the seals are airtight by pressing down on the lid of each jar; it should be rigid with a slight depression. If the lid is raised or you are able to pop the lid up and down with your finger, then the seal is not sound and the contents are not fit for storing.

Weighted-gauge pressure canner *Steam venting from vent* *Push down the lid to test the seal*

PRESSURE CANNING EQUIPMENT

Canning vegetables requires fairly minimal equipment. Pressure canners come in two types: dial-gauge or weighted-gauge canners. Dial-gauge canners allow for a more accurate reading and are generally considered more user friendly.

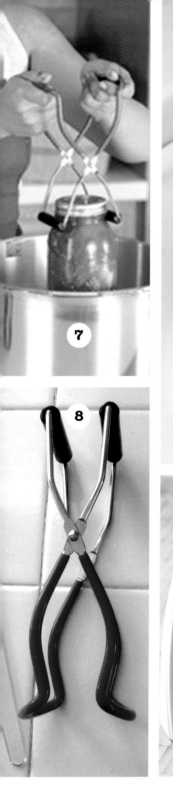

7

10

8

11

12

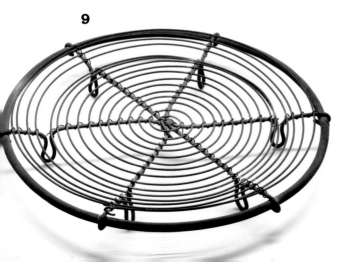

9

1: Canning jars (various sizes); 2 & 3: Self-sealing lids with rubberized gasket and metal screw bands; 4: Wide mouth funnel; 5: Spatula; 6: Dial-gauge pressure canner; 7 & 8: Jar lifter; 9: Cooling rack; 10: Magnetic lid handler; 11: Timer; 12: Screw band remover

STORING CANNED VEGETABLES

Storing canned vegetables properly will ensure that the vegetables will retain their fresh color and flavor. The jars should be stored upright in a cool, dry, dark place away from direct sunlight and heating pipes or vents. Before storing canned vegetables, remember to remove the screw bands around the lids, as the screw bands can rust and become difficult to remove later. The gasket on the lid forms a tight seal as it cools. If there is an issue with one of the jars, the lid will lift up, alerting you that bacteria may have developed. Leaving the screw bands in place could mean this will go undetected. Wipe the rims clean, and label and date the jars.

STORING FRESH VEGETABLES

Tender leafy greens, podded vegetables, and easily bruised vegetables such as bell peppers and summer squash begin to decline in quality as soon as they are harvested. They should be eaten as soon as possible; refrigerating either in an airtight container or loosely wrapped will help slow this process. Most

Canned vegetables stored in a cool cellar

vegetables stored in the refrigerator benefit from some additional moisture; others need to be stored dry, such as arugula, okra, and eggplant. Tomatoes should never be refrigerated or they will become mealy. Bulb, root, and tuberous vegetables, such as garlic, onions, potatoes, and sweet potatoes, do not require refrigeration and can be stored in a cool, dark, well-ventilated place. Few people today possess a root cellar or dedicated food storage beyond the refrigerator and kitchen cupboard, so these foods will do just as well in an unheated basement, cupboard, or pantry stored in a box and packed with sawdust or peat moss. Soil should be removed from root vegetables before storing, but they should not be washed. (Onions and potatoes should not be stored in close proximity, as the potatoes give off a gas that causes the onions to deteriorate.)

Potatoes stored in sacks

CHAPTER 1

LEAFY VEGETABLES, FLOWERS & BUDS

Cynara cardunculus var. *scolymus*

ARTICHOKE

The artichoke is an ancient species that originated in the Mediterranean. It is a perennial herbaceous plant belonging to the Asteraceae family. The tender edible part of the vegetable is found at the heart of a large unopened flower bud. Left to grow, this bud will open to produce a stunning violet-blue thistlelike flower, making this a popular choice for the garden and for use in ornamental displays.

Artichoke flower

Artichoke heart

Medicinal Uses

Both the tender edible part and the tough outer leaves of the artichoke have significant health benefits. The leaves are pressed and the pulp used to make a valuable extract. Artichoke has been found to have one of the highest levels of antioxidants in any vegetable; it contains the polyphenol-type antioxidants cynarin, rutin, quercetin, and gallic acid. Studies have shown that artichoke leaf extract can lower cholesterol levels, improve digestive health, relieve the symptoms of irritable bowel syndrome, and boost liver function.

A MANY-FACETED VEGETABLE

The artichoke is associated with Italian cuisine, but it is popular throughout Europe, North Africa, the Middle East, Asia Minor, and the United States. As a Mediterranean native, the artichoke thrives in warm, dry climates; in the United States, Monterey County in California is a major center for artichoke production. This vegetable is used in a wide array of dishes and preparations worldwide. In Vietnam artichoke is even dried and used as a tea, but perhaps its most elegant manifestation is as the main flavoring ingredient in the Italian liqueur Cynar.

Artichoke leaf extract

Cynar aperitif

Eruca sativa

ARUGULA

The deeply lobed leaves of the arugula plant are prized for their spicy, piquant flavor and have become a favored addition to salads and sandwiches. It is a fast-growing, high-yielding annual that originated in the Mediterranean, but has naturalized in temperate climates worldwide. In some English-speaking countries, arugula is known as "garden rocket" or simply "rocket."

SWEETEST IN THE SPRING

Arugula grows best in cool weather, and has a finer flavor when harvested while still young and tender. When the plant begins to produce flowers, it is an indication that it is nearing the end of its prime eating season and the leaves will taste bitter. Gardeners may opt to start afresh with a new planting to provide a second, warm-weather harvest in the fall. The flowers are also edible, with a similar peppery flavor. These appear on tall stems up to three feet in length.

Arugula in flower

Pretty arugula flowers garnish

Arugula leaves

SPICY INDEED

For the ancient Greeks and Romans, arugula was valued as an aphrodisiac believed to stimulate the libido and enliven the senses. It was planted around shrines of fertility gods such as Priapus. Lucius Junius Moderatus Columella makes this dedication in the first century AD: "Th'eruca, Priapus, near thee we sow, To arouse to duty husbands who are slow." Some of these beliefs may be borne out by science—arugula possesses high levels of essential vitamins, minerals, and powerful antioxidants that are known to lower blood pressure and increase blood flow. Arugula should also be remembered for itsulcer-fighting and anticancer properties, and its particular ability to cleanse pesticides and herbicides from the body.

Ancient Roman agriculturalist Lucius Junius Moderatus Columella

Ocimum basilicum

BASIL

Basil is a sun-loving, fast-growing, bushy annual native to Eurasia and Africa. It is grown for its edible leaves and for its use as an essential oil. It also has decorative appeal in the garden.

BASIL VARIETIES

This fragrant plant has been cultivated for centuries, and many forms have developed since its humble beginning. The basil plant comes in an array of different cultivars bred for their color, fragrance, habit, and ornamental features.

Clockwise: bush basil; purple basil; holy basil; Thai basil

Culinary Uses

The sweetly fragrant scent of this tender-leaved plant has many culinary applications in Europe and throughout Asia, both as a dried herb and as a salad leaf. It is the basis for two classic Italian dishes: *pasta con pesto* and the wonderfully simple *insalata Caprese*, a salad of sliced mozzarrella, sliced tomatoes, and whole basil leaves dressed with balsamic vinegar and olive oil. Asian basil is somewhat stronger-tasting with spicy notes and is used widely in stir-fry dishes and stews.

A SYMBOL OF FAITHFULNESS

The English poet John Keats's poem *Isabella, or the Pot of Basil* (1818) tells the story of a young Italian noblewoman who falls in love with a commoner, Lorenzo. Her family intends for her to marry a wealthy nobleman and forbids the relationship. When she learns that her brothers have murdered and buried her lover, Isabella exhumes his skull and keeps it in a pot planted with basil. She waters the plant with her tears and pines away. This rather macabre poem inspired a painting by the pre-Raphaelite artist William Holman Hunt, who depicted Isabella embracing the pot of basil.

Isabella and the Pot of Basil,
William Holman Hunt, 1868

Beta vulgaris ssp. *vulgaris*

BEET GREENS

The deep-red flesh and sweet flavor of the beetroot tends to overshadow the humble greens, but beet greens are also edible and delicious eaten raw in salads or cooked, much as you would prepare spinach. A cold-loving plant, beetroot is particularly popular in northern and eastern Europe.

TWO FOR THE PRICE OF ONE

Beet greens have been eaten since ancient times, and they have much to offer today. They are inexpensive, and if purchased still attached to beetroot they provide a second meal at no extra cost. They also pack a healthy punch, being high in iron, calcium, magnesium, vitamin A, and vitamin K, among others. For those who steer clear of dark leafy greens, smoothies are another way to go. Blended with bananas, pineapples, and orange juice, and flavored with vanilla or a little maple syrup, these refreshing, cheerfully colored drinks are easy on the stomach and a gentle way to introduce greens into the diet.

Bunch of beet greens

Baby beet greens

Green smoothie

Silene vulgaris

BLADDER CAMPION

This pretty flowering perennial is instantly recognizable for its delicately veined calyxes, which have the appearance of puff-sleeved blouses with frilly cuffs. In North America it is largely regarded as a weed, but in Europe, where it originated, it is still valued as a wild vegetable.

A FOOD IN LEAN TIMES

Bladder campion is widely eaten in the Mediterranean, and it is a particular favorite in Cyprus, where the plant is cultivated for commercial use. In Italy it is known as *silene* or *sculpit*; in Spain its leaves are called *collejas*, once used to make the dish *gazpacho viudo*, "widower gazpacho," so named for its use as a substitute for meat in times of scarcity. Both the shoots and leaves of bladder campion are edible. Young leaves have a sweet flavor and are a good addition to salads; the shoots are a little more bitter. Bladder campion can be found growing freely along roadsides and in meadows. The flowers emit a clovelike scent in the evening that attracts moths and makes an after-dinner stroll in the country all the more pleasurable.

A meadow plant

Moth feeding on bladder campion

Borago officinalis

BORAGE GREENS

A charming flowering herb also known as starflower, borage was cultivated in ancient times for its culinary and medicinal use. Today it is enjoyed primarily as a vegetable and as a dried herb, and it is valued in the garden for its ornamental qualities. Borage also attracts bees, who are always welcome in the garden (another name for it is "bee bread").

A DIAMOND IN THE ROUGH

Borage is a fast-growing, short-lived annual native to the Mediterranean, where it often grows freely as a weed. It has a loose, somewhat untidy form and an Old World appearance that is best suited to informal, wild gardens. The leaves are edible, with a faint cucumber flavor, but they are hairy and rough and are best chopped very small or used alongside

Rare white flowering borage

Pink borage flower

the flowers as a garnish. They can also impart flavor to liquids.

THE STAR FLOWER

Borage has soothing, mildly diuretic properties. Borage tea was long reputed to lift the spirits and alleviate melancholy. The pretty star-shaped flowers are often pink upon opening, before turning a vivid shade of blue. The flowers of borage are edible and are used traditionally as decorative embellishments for foods and drinks. The flowers can also be preserved as candied sweets and used to decorate cakes.

Borage in the garden

Brassica oleracea var. *italica*

BROCCOLI

It may come as no surprise that broccoli is closely related to cauliflower; they are cultivars of the same species within the large Brassicaceae, or cabbage family. Broccoli is native to the Mediterranean and it has played an important part in Italian cuisine dating as far back as the Roman Empire.

Broccoli cross-section

BROCCOLI FLORETS

When the outer leaves are removed from this plant it looks somewhat like a miniature tree, with a thick central trunk and smaller branches radiating outward. These branches are called florets, which in botanical terms refers to the cluster of small flowers that make up a composite flower head. The rough and knobby florets of the broccoli plant are parts of the flower head in its immature bud stage. The leaves and fleshy stems of the plant are edible, too, but generally only the florets are eaten. Three common types in wide production today are broccoli (properly named Calabrese broccoli after the Calabria region in Italy), purple broccoli, and sprouting broccoli.

Purple sprouting broccolis

Brassica oleracea var. *italica* x *alboglabra*

Broccolini

This diminutive, long-limbed version of broccoli is not baby broccoli as is sometimes thought—it is a hybrid of broccoli and Chinese broccoli (also known as Chinese kale) whose Cantonese name is *kai-lan*. Broccolini is a relatively new cultivar. It was developed in Japan in 1993 and debuted as broccolini in the United States five years later. It has a mild, sweet flavor, and tender flesh. Unlike broccoli, the whole vegetable is eaten, including the small yellow flowers that are sometimes found on the plant.

Broccolini flowers

Broccolini ready for the table

Culinary Uses

This simple, traditional Roman dish combines broccoli florets with garlic and red chili flakes. The ingredients are combined in a skillet, fried quickly and gently, and the whole dish is ready in just 2–3 minutes. As with all members of the Brassicaceae family, broccoli is very rich in nutrients, in particular vitamin C. Broccoli also contains antiviral, antibacterial, and anticancer properties. Boiling the vegetable greatly reduces these properties, but stir-frying, steaming, and microwaving methods allow them to remain intact.

Broccoli strascinati
(broccoli with garlic and hot pepper)

Brassica rapa ssp. *rapa*

BROCCOLI RABE

Broccoli rabe (sometimes called "rapini" in the U.S.) has many names around the world, which can be confusing, since it looks like broccoli, has broccoli in its name, but is not in fact closely related to broccoli. It is in the same subspecies as the turnip (in Italy it is called *cime di rapi*, "turnip tops") and it bears similar leaves to turnip greens.

SMALL BUT POWERFUL

This dark green, bitter-tasting vegetable is a great favorite in Italy, especially around Rome and in the Italian south, but it is also widely eaten in Portugal and China. The whole plant is edible, including the little yellow flowers that may have opened on the small budded florets. Like all Brassicas, broccoli rabe is a power vegetable, very high in vitamin A and C and loaded with other healthful benefits. It is a fast-growing biennial generally grown as an annual.

Clockwise: fresh broccoli rabe; broccoli rabe with flowers; steamed broccoli rabe; a garden harvest

Brassica oleracea ssp. *gemmifera*

BRUSSELS SPROUTS

Cruciform flower

As the name suggests, Brussels sprouts were first cultivated in Belgium, in the region then known as Flanders. The first recorded mention of the vegetable is in 1587, but they may have been cultivated there as early as the 1200s. The thick, upright stem of this plant bears many miniature cabbagelike heads along its entire length. The stalks can reach up to three feet in height.

LOVE THEM OR LOATHE THEM

Brussels sprouts have a strong flavor and can be bitter tasting (and bad smelling) if overcooked. This has caused a dubious reputation for Brussels sprouts, so much so that a survey conducted in 2008 named Brussels sprouts America's "most-hated vegetable." They are avoided by children and adults alike. This is unfortunate because Brussels sprouts have many admirable qualities; cooked properly, they are a delicious, versatile vegetable that can be eaten raw in salads, or boiled, steamed, roasted, grilled, or fried. As a member of the Brassicaceae family, they are also packed with nutrients and beneficial properties.

Growing characteristics

*Harvested
Brussels sprouts*

Loose Brussels sprouts

A BRITISH FAVORITE

Despite being the bane of British schoolchildren faced with soggy Brussels sprouts in the school dining room, the British nonetheless eat more Brussels sprouts than anyone else in Europe. This reaches a peak during the winter holiday season, when Brussels sprouts are sold—by the millions—as an essential component of the Christmas dinner, where they are often paired with chestnuts. Although they are ranked among America's most hated foods, Brussels sprouts enjoy some popularity in the U.S. with health-conscious individuals who want to boost their intake of protein, iron, potassium, vitamin C, folate, and fiber.

*Brussels sprouts
and chestnuts*

Brassica oleracea ssp. *capitata*

CABBAGE

The king of the Brassicaceae family, cabbage is eaten across the globe and appears in many different culinary guises. Cabbage is available in many varieties, the most common being the smooth white variety, but colors can be white, green, purple, and red, and the leaves range from smooth to crimped.

A HEAD OF CABBAGE

The compact, tightly formed cabbages we are familiar with today are cultivars of the wild ancestral form, which was more open-leaved and did not produce a head (the word *cabbage* is derived from the Old French word *caboche*, meaning "head"). Modern cultivars have been developed for their high yields and head weight, which range between one to nine pounds. As of 2012 the world record weight for a cabbage was 138.25 pounds. Cabbage is a biennial plant, producing a large, dense head of leaves in its first year.

Savoy cabbage

Smooth white cabbage

Ornamental cabbage

THE CABBAGE IN ART

Cabbage was an important food in the Middle Ages, and it was a staple food for the poor in lean times. The austere still life paintings of the Spanish artist Juan Sánchez Cotán, painted at the turn of the seventeenth century, pay homage to the cabbage.

Quince, Cabbage, Melon and Cucumber, *Juan Sánchez Cotán, 1602*

CABBAGE & KALE GALLERY

Cabbage and kale cultivars have become highly popular as ornamental plants, prized for their great variety of color, form, and texture.

1: Mixed ornamental cabbage and kale; 2: Pink and white bicolor kale; 3: White Peacock ornamental cabbage; 4: Yellow smooth leaf cabbage; 5: Red ornamental cabbage; 6: Ornamental cabbage; 7: Flowering ornamental kale

Capparis spinosa

CAPERS

This tough, drought-tolerant shrubby plant is best known for its piquant flower buds. The small green buds—capers—are salted or pickled and used to season foods the world over, especially in the Mediterranean. The caper bush, or *Capparis spinosa*, grows abundantly in hot, dry countries.

Caper plant buds

Mature caper berry with seeds

WITHOUT EQUAL

Capers are marketed in six sizes; the smallest, nonpareil caper, is considered the finest, and they decrease in value the larger they become. In order to qualify as a nonpareil caper, the bud must measure no more than 7 mm across. Other categories respectively are surfines, capucines, capotes, fines, and lastly, grusas, which measure a hefty 14 mm or more. If left on the bush, caper buds will mature into flowers and develop fruit—the caper berry. Edible caper berries are harvested when they are roughly the size of a large olive, and they are also salted or pickled.

Harvested capers

Salted capers

Caper flower

A TROPICAL BEAUTY

The native origins of the caper bush are unknown; however, the exotic form of the caper flower would certainly look at home in a tropical environment. Rounded, pinkish-white petals surround a large single stigma and multiple delicate purple stamens. The flowers are short-lived, lasting only one day. They are also edible, but are generally reserved for decoration.

Brassica oleracea var. *botrytis*

CAULIFLOWER

Another member of the Brassicaceae, or cabbage family, the cauliflower is a popular vegetable eaten throughout Europe, North America, and Asia. Its name is a compound of the Latin word *caulis*, meaning "cabbage," and the modern English word "flower." The leaves and stalk are edible, but typically only the white florets are eaten.

A PALE BEAUTY

The white part of the cauliflower plant is actually the inflorescence (or bud) in an undeveloped state. The flesh of the vegetable is white because the leaves of the plant curl over the top of the head while it grows, protecting it from the sun and preventing the production of chlorophyll. If left alone, the plant will continue to grow and develop flowers. It is believed that this plant was first eaten in Asia Minor, then in Italy,

before it made its way to other parts of Europe. It wasn't cultivated in North America until the beginning of the twentieth century. Many different varieties of cauliflower have been developed, and today more cauliflowers are produced in China than anywhere else.

A MATHEMATICAL VEGETABLE

Romanesco broccoli is a form of cauliflower. The beautiful, somewhat bizarre patterns formed by the swirling structure of this vegetable are a naturally occurring mathematical set. They conform to fractal patterns, in which patterns are replicated on all scales throughout a structure. In addition, the number of swirls on each head of Romanesco conforms to the Fibonacci mathematical sequence, in which each number is the sum of the two previous numbers.

Head of Romanesco

Colorful cauliflower cultivars

Distinctive Romanesco patterns

Cichorium intybus

CHICORY

Common chicory is a fast-growing perennial of the Asteraceae family that bears pretty, blue, daisylike flowers. It has a long history as a medicinal plant. Today we are more familiar with the numerous cultivars of this plant that have been developed for culinary use as leafy salad vegetables.

COFFEE SUBSTITUTE

All parts of the common chicory plant are edible, including the milk sap and taproot. The taproot can be roasted, ground, and used as a caffeine-free, less expensive substitute for coffee.

Roasted chicory root

CAMP

REGD. TRADE MARK.

READY AYE READY

CHICORY & COFFEE ESSENCE
with added sugar

241 ml e

SL 1300/1

great to use in baking

Coffee substitute

Cichorium intybus

Belgian Endive

One of the most popular cultivars of common chicory is Belgian endive. Its tightly packed, smoothly tapered form bears little resemblance to loose-leaf chicories. Belgian endive was developed as a result of happenstance after chicory roots were discovered to produce pale leaves in a darkened cellar. Commercial Belgian endive is grown completely in the dark to maintain the yellowish white color of its leaves (its name in Dutch, witloof, means "white leaf"). It is relatively easy to grow at   home covered in black plastic or kept in a dark place.

"White leaf" endive

Wild chicory

Chrysanthemum coronarium

CHRYSANTHEMUM LEAVES

All chrysanthemum flowers are edible, but they vary in flavor from mild and sweet to sharp and bitter. The flowers can be added to salads for a decorative finish, stir-fried, infused as a tea, or made into wine. *Chrysanthemum coronarium*, also known as chrysanthemum greens, is an herbaceous annual of the Asteraceae family. It is the most palatable variety of chrysanthemum and its leafy greens are particularly popular in Asian cuisine.

Wild garland chrysanthemums

Culinary Uses

Chrysanthemum leaves may be found by the bunch in Asian supermarkets or some specialty stores in the United States. Young leaves can be added to salads, but, as their bitterness increases with age, larger leaves are best lightly steamed. The bitter, grassy flavor of chrysanthemum leaves pairs especially well with the sweet, nutty flavor of sesame sauce.

Brassica oleracea

COLLARD GREENS

Perhaps more than any other leafy green vegetable, collard greens are closely associated with the southern United States. Native to Asia Minor, collard greens are also a staple food in Brazil, Portugal, India, and East Africa.

ROSETTE FORM

This plant does not develop a head like other members of the Brassicaceae, or cabbage family. It grows in a loose-leaved rosette form and, like spinach, both stalks and leaves are eaten. Collard greens are thick, dark blue-green in hue, and have a slightly bitter, robust flavor. The large leaves are heavily veined, and the tough lower parts are trimmed before eating. As a hardy and also heat-tolerant plant, it is grown year-round in southern parts of the United States.

Rosette form

Culinary Uses

One of the best-known, best-loved dishes eaten throughout the southern United States is a simple but flavorful preparation—called simply collard greens—which combines the dark green leaves with smoked meats (such as bacon, ham, or turkey), and onion and garlic. Vegetarian versions of this dish often pair collard greens with black-eyed peas.

Caldo verde
(Portuguese green soup)

Southern style collard greens

Collard greens with bacon

Medicinal Uses

Collard greens contain high levels of vitamin K; one cup provides significantly more than the recommended daily amount. Vitamin K is essential for healthy bones, as it helps the body absorb and retain calcium. The high level of chlorophyll in collard greens, which accounts for its dark green hue, is also known to help protect against the carcinogenic properties of heterocyclic amines (HCAs). HCAs result from a chemical reaction in meats that are cooked at high temperatures. This is a particular consideration for people who regularly enjoy barbecued, chargrilled, or well-done meats. Eating collard greens alongside these foods can help offset these negative effects.

Lepidium sativum

CRESS

Cress is a small, peppery-tasting plant grown for its sprouts, seeds, and oil. It is a member of the Brassicaceae family and is related to mustard and watercress. It is a fast-growing plant that can grow from seed to table in as little as seven days. This makes it a particularly useful learning tool in the classroom or at home.

TRADITIONAL MEDICINE

Cress seeds are high in folic acid and iron, which are helpful in the treatment of iron-deficiency anemia and in boosting the body's immunity. Cress seeds have long been used in traditional medicines in India. Chewing the seeds can soothe respiratory discomfort, and the seeds have bronco-dilating qualities that can help relieve bronchitis and asthma. Cress seeds are also used in traditional medicine as a natural alternative to pharmaceutical expectorants.

Cress seeds

Culinary Uses

Cress sprouts are a popular crop in northern Europe. The peppery flavor of cress is a favorite of the British, especially when combined with savory egg salad to create the teatime classic, egg and cress sandwiches.

Traditional English tea sandwich

Taraxacum officinale

DANDELION

The common dandelion may be an unwelcome sight in a carefully manicured lawn, but it has a long history as a nutritional food source and as a valuable medicinal plant—not to mention its contribution to dandelion wine.

A DANDELION A DAY

This tough little plant contains over half the recommended daily amount of vitamin C, and it is one of the richest sources of vitamins A and K of any culinary herb. It is also packed with flavonoids and the minerals magnesium, potassium, calcium, and iron.

Medicinal Uses

Dandelion has been used for centuries as an herbal medicine. The first half of its botanical name, *Taraxacum*, is a compound of Latin words that loosely translate as "disorder" and "remedy." The second half, *officinale*, is a word whose modern equivalent is "pharmacy," and it denotes its standing as a medicinal plant. It was used to treat various illnesses identified in the Middle Ages, such as itching, boils, toothache, gallstones, and jaundice. Today dandelion is valued for its positive impact on the digestive system and as a natural liver cleanser. As such, it can be helpful in counteracting some of the negative effects of prescription medicines. Its mildly diuretic action also makes it useful in treating problems associated with water retention.

French apothecary (15th century)

Roasted dandelion root

Hemerocallis fulva

DAYLILY

The daylily produces abundant dusty-orange colored flowers that last for only one day. In the United States (where it is also called roadside daylily and outhouse lily) it can be seen growing freely along roadsides. Its vigorous and invasive habit, combined with its ability to grow almost anywhere, means that some people regard it as a weed.

PRETTY AND VERSATILE

The daylily is such a familiar sight in the United States that it is often mistakenly believed to be a native species, but it was introduced from Asia to the United States at the end of the nineteenth century. Today over 40,000 cultivars are available. The flowers, tuberous roots, and buds of the daylily are edible. The flowers have a pleasant, slightly spicy taste. They can be eaten raw in salads or sautéed, steamed, and added to soups and stews, and they make a particularly dazzling edible garnish. Like summer squash, the flowers can also be battered and deep-fried.

Harvested daylily buds

Colorful cultivars

WARNING! The edible common daylily should not be confused with lilies of a different genus, as many of those are toxic to animals and humans.

Anethum graveolens

DILL

Dill is an aromatic herb prized in kitchens around the world. It is a member of the sprawling Apiaceae family, which also includes parsley, carrot, celery, and fennel. Originally native to Southwest Asia, dill has naturalized throughout Europe and the northern United States.

THE SOOTHING HERB

The name of this plant is thought to derive from an Old Norse word, *dilla*, which means "to lull." Dill is commonly used to ease stomach discomfort, and it is an ingredient in gripe water, given to sooth colicky babies. It is valued in the garden as an ornamental annual with wispy blue-green leaves and scented yellow flowers that open on wide umbels, which are a distinctive feature of this species. Flowering dill attracts many beneficial insects into the garden, and it is an important food source for Swallowtail butterfly larva.

Swallowtail butterfly on dill plant

Dill in the garden

Culinary Uses

Dill is one of the most popular herbs in eastern Europe and Scandinavian countries. Both the leaves and seeds of this plant are widely used in sauces, pickles, and as garnish. It is particularly favored as an accompaniment to fish.

Notable dishes include:

Gravlax: a Nordic dish prepared with cured raw salmon and served cold with a dill and mustard sauce.

Dill pickles: salt-brined or fermented pickled cucumbers seasoned with dill, usually served as an accompaniment to sandwiches.

Gravlax with dill

Clockwise: dill leaves; dill seeds; dill flowers

Cichorium endivia

ENDIVE

Endive (*Cichorium endivia*) is often confused with the smooth white Belgian endive (*Cichorium intybus*) but it is, in fact, a separate cultivar of common chicory, and it is similar in shape and habit to lettuce. There are two kinds of endive, the frilly, tightly curled frisée and the broad-leaved escarole.

SOUPS AND SALADS

Frisée is grown almost exclusively as a salad vegetable, where it contributes interesting texture and color to dishes. Escarole, on the other hand, is used both as a salad leaf and in soups and other warm dishes. It is particularly popular in the Mediterranean. Both types are slightly bitter. To achieve attractive pale leaves at the center of a frisée head, it is customary to loosely tie or place an elastic band around the midsection of the plant up to one week before harvesting. The "blanched" inner leaves will be more tender as a result.

Frisée tied with string

Blanched interior

Mixed endive leaves

Escarole soup

Diplazium esculentum

FIDDLEHEAD

Diplazium esculentum is a forest-dwelling edible fern that originated in the East and has naturalized throughout Asia and Oceania. The edible parts of vegetable fern are aptly named; the attractive, tightly curled whorls of the immature fronds closely resemble the scroll on a fiddle.

A SPRING DELICACY

Fiddleheads are eaten while young and tender. They are harvested in early spring, just as the ferns begin to emerge from the undergrowth. They are a popular vegetable throughout East and Southeast Asia, with a nutty flavor akin to asparagus. In North America the most common species of edible fern is the ostrich fern. Historically valued in the United States primarily for their ornamental use, ferns are growing in popularity as a vegetable (although there is a long tradition of foraging in northeastern parts of the country). Ferns are rarely cultivated for commercial use; they are primarily a foraging plant.

Forest ferns

Culinary Uses

Widely used in Asian cuisines in stir-fried dishes, soups, and stews, fiddleheads are generally served cooked to counteract any bitterness. They are also enjoyed as a pickled vegetable, which greatly extends their season. Recipes for pickled fiddleheads are relatively simple. The fiddleheads are washed thoroughly, then boiled for 10–15 minutes to improve flavor and kill any toxins. Then they are combined with vinegar, sugar, salt, and various other seasonings depending on the region, and sealed in a pickling jar.

A fancy addition to quiche

WARNING! Care must be taken not to confuse these edible ferns with nonedible poisonous types, including bracken, which is carcinogenic. Brackens are identified by their coarse, highly divided comblike leaves.

Bracken fronds

Houttuynia cordata

FISH MINT

The name of this edible leafy plant may help to explain its lack of use as a culinary plant in the United States. It is grown in the United States primarily as groundcover, where it is commonly known as chameleon plant or rainbow plant. It is favored for its pretty, often variegated, heart-shaped leaves, small white flowers, and also for its tolerance for shady, damp areas. It is fast-growing and can become invasive.

BIG IN JAPAN

The leaves of this plant have a strong fishy aroma. It is especially popular in Vietnam as an accompaniment to grilled meats and fish-based dishes, and it is also eaten in northeast India, Japan, and China. The Cantonese name for *Houttuynia cordata* translates as "fishy-smell herb." In Japan it is called *dokudami*, which means "poison blocking," so named for its antibacterial, antiviral, and anti-inflammatory properties. It is used as a traditional medicine in both Japan and China, and is widely available processed as an herbal extract.

Fish mint flowers

Variegated leaf variety

Houttuynia extract

The roots of the fish mint plant are a popular dish in China

Telfairia occidentalis

FLUTED PUMPKIN

Fluted pumpkin—so named for the deep parallel ridges on its fruit—is a fast-growing tropical vine belonging to the Cucurbitaceae family. Fluted pumpkin is a widely consumed vegetable valued for its nutritious leaves and copious seeds. It is native to West Africa, but is extensively cultivated in Nigeria.

GIANT FRUITS

Hanging from trellises, the fruits of *Telfairia occidentalis* have the appearance of large bellows. These enormous fruits can grow up to 40 inches in length and an individual fruit can weigh as much as 40 pounds. The fruit itself is not edible, but it contains many large, red seeds that are an important source of protein. Boiled seeds are eaten whole and used in the traditional Nigerian soup *edikang ikong*, or made into a fermented porridge. Roasted seeds are ground to make bread. The fragrant young shoots and leaves are widely used as a green vegetable and potherb. The leaves of the fluted pumpkin are rich in vitamin C, iron, and potassium, and they also have antioxidant and antimicrobial properties. The leaves are prepared as a natural medicine used to purify the blood.

Fluted pumpkin flower

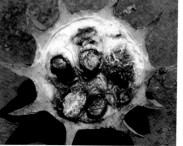

Fluted pumpkin seeds

59

Brassica oleracea ssp. *acephala*

KALE

Smooth leaf kale

Curly kale

This hearty green vegetable is part of the Brassicaceae family, which includes cabbage, Brussels sprouts, cauliflower, and broccoli. Unlike cabbage, kale produces erect stems with wavy or crinkly leaves, but has a rosette of leaves rather than a compact head at the center. It is a very hardy plant and can continue to be harvested through the snow; in fact, the flavor improves when kale has been exposed to frost, which triggers the plant to convert some of its starch into sugars.

Kale in the snow

LONG LIVE KALE

One of the earliest vegetables to be cultivated by humans, kale has been around for centuries. It was a staple green vegetable in Europe during the Middle Ages before eventually being superseded by cabbage. Although other cultivars in this family have been modified over time, kale eaten today bears close resemblance to its primitive forms. English settlers introduced kale to North America in the seventeenth century; in the twenty-first century it has risen again in popularity as a healthy and versatile vegetable. The most common form of kale today is curly kale, or Scots kale.

Culinary Uses

For the uninitiated and young children who might look askance at the decidedly good-for-you appearance of kale, there are ways to prepare it that will tempt even the most doubtful. Baked kale chips are quick and easy to make, require minimal ingredients (just kale leaves, olive oil, and a touch of salt), and they have all of the crunchy appeal of regular chips without the downsides.

Homemade kale chips

Medicinal Uses

There is no debate about the high nutritional content in kale; it is simply one of the healthiest leafy green vegetables out there. It is extremely high in vitamin K and C—a cup of raw kale contains twice as much vitamin C as an orange! It is high in beta-carotene and other powerful antioxidants, which are known to have positive effects on the immune system. It contains calcium, potassium, magnesium, and essential minerals that are necessary to good health. It can also help to lower cholesterol levels in the body.

Power pack

Valerianella locusta

LAMB'S LETTUCE

This diminutive leaf vegetable is commonly known as lamb's lettuce or corn salad. It is also known by its French name, *mache*. Lamb's lettuce was a forage food long before it was cultivated in France in the seventeenth century. Its English name is derived from its slightly spoon-shaped leaves, which are thought to resemble a lamb's tongue.

SIGNS OF SPRING

Lamb's lettuce is a cool-weather plant. Unlike many salad vegetables it is surprisingly hardy, and it is one of the first vegetables to appear after winter is over.

A TENDER ALTERNATIVE

For people who don't enjoy the bitter tang that characterizes many salad vegetables, lamb's lettuce is a natural choice. Its leaves are very tender with a sweet, slightly nutty taste. Their tenderness makes them challenging to market as they are easily bruised and have a relatively short shelf life. Keeping the price down is a challenge since lamb's lettuce is labor-intensive to gather—it is a low-growing plant that cannot be mechanically harvested.

Spring lamb

First signs of spring

A GERMAN FAIRY TALE

Another common name for lamb's lettuce is field salad, which in Germany is called *rapunzel*. In the Brothers' Grimm fairy tale, Rapunzel's expectant mother is overcome with a craving for the tender leaves that she sees growing nearby in a sorceress's garden. She persuades her husband to steal some for her and when he is caught red-handed, he is forced to barter their unborn child in return. When the sorceress comes to claim the child, she names her Rapunzel after the plant.

Commemorative stamp

Bowl of lamb's lettuce

Lactuca sativa

LETTUCE

Lettuce is the most common salad leaf consumed worldwide. The ancient Egyptians first cultivated lettuce millennia ago, most likely from prickly weed lettuce, *Lactuca serriola*. Today, innumerable varieties of lettuce are available globally, with China in the lead in terms of production.

Culinary Uses

The word *lettuce* is a derivation of the Latin word *lactuca*, the name given to it by the ancient Romans. One of the most celebrated lettuce dishes of all is not named for ancient Roman royalty, as might be supposed, but for Caesar Cardini, who invented it in 1924. Caesar salad is a simple but satisfying combination of crisp romaine lettuce, pungent anchovies, and creamy mayonnaise finished with grated Parmesan cheese.

There are many slight variations of the dish.

Romaine lettuce

Caesar salad

A KITCHEN GARDEN

Lettuce is an easy, fast-growing plant that favors cool conditions. It also does well in containers, so it is a good choice for small yards, balconies, and even window boxes. Containers have the added advantage of being closer to the kitchen and situated away from animals that might want to eat them.

Potted romaine

Clockwise: iceberg lettuce; mixed loose leaf salad; stem lettuce

LETTUCE GALLERY

There are just a few types of lettuce, but hundreds of cultivars, each developed for its particular flavor, texture, size, color, or ease of growing.

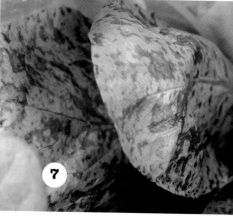

1: Butterhead lettuce; 2: Stem lettuce;
3: Mignonette; 4: Lollo Rosso; 5: Romaine;
6: Boston bib; 7: Speckled trout

Brassica, Sinapis

MUSTARD

The Brassicaceae family contains numerous species of mustard plant that fall into two genera: *Brassica* and *Sinapis*. Mustard is grown primarily for its copious seeds, but also for its leafy greens. The pale seeds of *Sinapis alba*, or white mustard, are used to make the popular condiment of the same name. *Brassica nigra*, or black mustard, produces black seeds, which are more pungent and produce a hotter mustard. Many vineyards in Sonoma County, California, have a burst of yellow appear near the end of winter due to mustard growing wild, or purposely planted, between the dormant grape trunks. Once buds break on the trunks, the mustard is mulched into the soil to provide valuable nutrients to the emerging gravevines.

SOME LIKE IT HOT

The pungent quality of mustard is due to the levels of sinalbin in the seeds. Ripe mustard seeds are hard and round. After harvesting, these are milled to make powdered mustard or mixed with liquids to make a paste. Whole mustard seeds are added to the vinegars of pickled foods to improve the flavor; their useful antibacterial properties also inhibit the growth of mold and bacteria. In Mediterranean countries the young leaves of the mustard plant are eaten as a salad vegetable and as a potherb. The leaves and flowers have a fresh, peppery taste. The leaves can also be braised as greens and added to soups and stews.

Clockwise: A patchwork landscape; mustard seeds; prepared mustard

Brassica rapa ssp. *chinensis*

PAK CHOY (Bok Choy)

Pak choy, one of many subspecies of *Brassica rapa*, originated in Southeast Asia and it has been cultivated in China for centuries. It was introduced to Europe in the nineteenth century, and it arrived in the United States around 1900, where it has become better-known as "bok choy."

CHINESE CABBAGE

In appearance more akin to celery, pak choy bears little resemblance to the round, compact forms we may associate with cabbage. Pak choy produces bladelike leaves in a loose rosette form. The leaf-to-stalk ratio differs from European cabbage varieties; the fleshy white stalks take up the larger part of the plant, while the dark green leaves are relatively diminutive. The stalks of pak choy have a mild flavor and a refreshingly crisp, juicy texture, which offsets the more robust flavor of the leaves.

Brassica rapa ssp. *pekinensis*

Napa Cabbage

The oblong, tightly formed napa cabbage (or *siu choi* in Cantonese) is another subspecies of *Brassica rapa,* or Chinese cabbage. It is a staple food in China, Japan, and Korea, and wherever there are large Chinese populations. In Korea it is the main ingredient used to make kimchi, a national dish made of spicy, fermented napa cabbage, seasoned with chili peppers and other pungent herbs and vegetables.

Kimchi is a very healthy food with many beneficial properties; it is considered an essential part of Korean culinary life and is eaten at almost every meal.

Head of napa cabbage

PARSLEY

Petroselinum crispum

Parsley is a biennial of the Apiaceae family, grown as an herb and a vegetable. The two most common types are Italian flat-leaf parsley and curly parsley. Less well-known is root parsley, which is similar in appearance to parsnip and tastes a little like celery.

AN ANCIENT CLASSIC

Native to the Mediterranean, parsley is widely used throughout Europe, the Middle East, Brazil, and the United States. A classic Middle Eastern dish is the Lebanese parsley salad tabbouleh, which combines parsley, tomatoes, bulgur wheat, mint, garlic, lemon, and olive oil. Flat-leaf parsley is used more often in cooked dishes, as it retains its flavor in the process. However, in parts of Europe curly parsley is favored over flat-leaf because of the latter's close resemblance to fool's parsley, a highly poisonous member of the same Apiaceae family, which can be fatal if ingested. Another flat-leaf relative of parsley is the aromatic herb cilantro, also known as Chinese parsley.

Clockwise: tabbouleh, curly parsley, cilantro

Pisum sativum

PEA SHOOTS

Pea shoots are the young growth of the edible pea plant, harvested before the plant fully matures and produces its fruit—the green peas found packed tightly inside the pea pod. All parts of the plant are edible and may also be grown just for the shoots, leaves and tendrils. The shoots can be used in salads and sautéed as greens; the young stems and leaves make a refreshing alternative to spinach.

LEAFLESS VARIETIES

There are many varieties of this annual vegetable, including semi-leafless and leafless cultivars in which leaves are replaced by clumps of wiry tendrils. These are especially popular among gardeners who wish to grow the plant primarily for its shoots and tendrils; the tendrils are sweeter and more tender than the shoots, which can become woody and stringy as the plant matures. The curly tendrils also make an unusual and attractive garnish.

WARNING!
The pretty blossoms of the edible pea plant have a pleasant mild pea flavor, not to be confused with the ornamental sweet pea species *Lathyrus odoratus*, which is poisonous.

*Flowering
pea plant*

*Sweet pea
blossoms*

Portulaca oleracea

PURSLANE

Depending on your geographic location, this pretty, small-leaved succulent is regarded either as a weed or enjoyed as a food. It grows abundantly in sunny parts of the world and bears modest yellow flowers. Cultivars of purslane are available with larger fancy blossoms in a variety of colors.

EDIBLE GROUNDCOVER

One of the few fast-growing annual succulents, this little plant is easy to grow, brings a lemony zest to summer salads, and it is packed with omega-3 fatty acids—more than any other edible plant. Its stems and thick leaves can also be fried or added to soups and stews, where its mucilaginous action serves as a thickener. Purslane is drought-tolerant and adaptable to all kinds of soils, and it is self-propagating. It produces abundant tiny seeds that are released from cone-shaped pods clustered on the stems. The seeds are edible and can be sown directly into the ground after the last frost. In the garden it is especially useful as edging or groundcover for difficult dry areas. It also grows well in rock gardens and looks pretty tumbling over stone walls.

Seedpods

Colorful purslane cultivars

Cichorium intybus
RADICCHIO

Radicchio is a subspecies of chicory, distinguishable by its variegated leaves and irregular shape. It was cultivated in northern Italy as far back as the fifteenth century (it is also known as Italian chicory). The thick, heavily veined, dark red leaves of radicchio resemble a small cabbage at first glance, but radicchio is grown as a leafy green and used primarily in salads.

EDIBLE BOWLS

Raw radicchio has a spicy, fairly bitter taste; tossing the leaves in salt, can help alleviate the bitterness. The leaves are so firm that they can serve as wraps or as edible bowls. Single leaves can be used to hold appetizers, or an entire head can be hollowed out to contain a small salad. Cooking radicchio sweetens the flavor; during cooking the color changes from red to deep brown.

Edible radicchio bowl

Colorful radicchio leaves

Rumex acetosa

SORREL

Common or garden sorrel, often known simply as sorrel, is a narrow-leaved plant with a sharp, lemony taste, which makes it popular as a salad green. It can also be steamed or braised as a leafy green and added to soups or stews. Sorrel is also known as sour dock and narrow-leaved dock.

WILD SORREL

Sorrel is a cold-hardy, drought-tolerant perennial native to the British Isles, and it grows best in temperate climates. It belongs to a genus of plants that also contains dock weed, the traditional remedy for painful hives caused by contact with stinging nettles. Sorrel can often be seen growing wild along roadsides, grasslands, and at woodland edges. Two other species suitable for the kitchen garden are French sorrel (*Rumex scutatus*) and blood sorrel (*Rumex sanguineus*). Blood sorrel, as its name suggests, has striking red-veined leaves and adds ornamental value as a garden plant. Sorrel is wind-pollinated and if allowed to produce seed, this plant can become invasive and difficult to control. Seeds are borne on tall flower spikes in early summer.

Blood sorrel

Wild sorrel

Spinacia oleracea

SPINACH

Spinach is a highly popular vegetable with a well-deserved reputation as a nutritious food. It is used equally as a salad leaf and leafy green vegetable, and it can be steamed, braised, and added to innumerable cooked dishes.

ANCIENT LINEAGE

Spinach was first cultivated thousands of years ago in Persia. By the sixth century it was being grown in China, and in medieval Europe it was a staple food. It came to the United States relatively late, arriving with European settlers. There are two basic types of spinach, curly leaf and smooth leaf, but there are many cultivars of these types developed for their hardiness, disease resistance, flavor, and ease of growing. Spinach is a cool-weather vegetable and does best in spring and fall; in the heat of midsummer the plant tends to "bolt" and divert its energy into producing flowers.

Container spinach

Spinach flowers

Culinary Uses

The word "Florentine" on a menu usually is synonymous with spinach. In Florence, Italy, spinach was historically associated with the aristocracy, and this association between the leaf and the location has persisted. A classic spinach dish in Greece is *spanakopita*, or spinach pie. This dish provides a wonderful contrast in texture and flavor; a filling of savory spinach mixed with feta cheese, onions, and seasonings is topped with flaky, buttery filo pastry.

POPEYE THE SAILOR MAN

Famously promoted for its high iron content, spinach is not actually the top leafy green in terms of its nutritional heft, but it is close. It belongs to the Brassicaceae family, which contains many dark green leafy vegetables packed with antioxidants, minerals, and vitamins, and the health benefits from eating these foods are many. The fictional character Popeye attributed his great strength to spinach, and he became a role model for healthy eating.

A roadside attraction

Cucurbita

SUMMER SQUASH BLOSSOMS

Zucchini and squash are species of herbaceous vine generally referred to as summer squash. They belong to the Cucurbitaceae, or gourd family, which also contains pumpkins and the colorfully varied winter squash.

A DELICATE TREAT

The large and surprisingly fleshy blossoms produced by these plants are edible and considered a treat. However, they are extremely perishable, and due to their short shelf life they are not often available in grocery stores. Fortunately, the squash is a relatively easy vegetable to grow in the garden.

Zucchini flowers

 Culinary Use
Squash blossoms can be eaten raw or they can be deep-fried, pan-fried, baked, added into soups, quesadillas, and pasta dishes, and prepared in a host of other ways. One of the most popular ways is to stuff squash blossoms with seasoned ricotta, dip them in batter, and deep-fry them for just a few minutes until golden brown.

Deep-fried squash blossoms

Beta vulgaris ssp. *cicla*

SWISS CHARD

Swiss chard is a high-fiber, nutrient-rich food native to the Mediterranean and closely related to the beetroot; they are both in the *Beta* genus. The red veins and stems of Swiss chard are the same deep red as the beetroot, but Swiss chard does not develop a taproot, so only the leaves are eaten.

EAT THE RAINBOW

The large, deeply veined, crinkly leaves of this plant make an attractive addition to salads, but it can also be added to soups or cooked as a leaf vegetable in its own right. There are many colorful cultivars of Swiss chard, developed for their added visual appeal, without compromising flavor. The most striking cultivar is perhaps Rainbow Swiss chard— the leaves range from green to bronze with multicolored stems that emerge in a dazzling rosette pattern.

Ruby Swiss chard

Rainbow Swiss chard

SWISS CHARD GALLERY

The irresistible ornamental appeal of colorful Swiss chard cultivars does not compromise their nutritional content, flavor, or ease of growing.

1

2

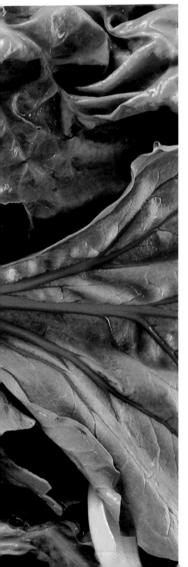

1: Pink chard; 2: Rainbow chard;
3: Rhubarb chard 4: White giant;
5: Canary yellow

Brassica rapa ssp. *rapa*

TURNIP GREENS

The leaves of the turnip plant can be eaten in addition to the root—the turnip. Like collard greens, turnip greens are popular in the southern United States, often served alongside smoked meats, although turnip greens are a little sweeter than their hearty cousins. The bulbous part of the turnip plant is actually a taproot, a large primary root that grows vertically downward and bears smaller lateral roots.

AN EITHER/OR FOOD

In the U.S., turnip leaves are generally called turnip greens; in the UK they are known as "turnip tops." Harvesting the "tops" too heavily for food will discourage root growth, so gardeners may decide to divide their crop so that some plants provide leafy greens and others provide the root vegetable. The leaves should be harvested when still small and tender, as larger leaves can be bitter (the bitterness can be reduced by changing the water during cooking after the first pan of water has boiled). The tender leaves have a sweet, slightly peppery flavor, and they are packed full of nutrients— several times more than the turnip root.

Fresh turnip greens

Cooked turnip leaves

Nasturtium officinale

WATERCRESS

Watercress is a member of the mustard family (properly known as the Brassicaceae family). It is cultivated as a leafy green used in salads and also in soups and stews. Its distinctive hot, peppery taste complements bland foods and enlivens meats.

A FLOATING CROP

Watercress grows naturally in water or in boggy places, kept afloat by hollow stems. Today, much commercially produced watercress is grown hydroponically. It is a highly perishable plant with a limited shelf life. Hydroponically produced plants are sold with the roots intact, which considerably increases its longevity. Its cousin land cress (also known as American cress) is a less water-dependent, easy-to-grow plant that is an acceptable substitute when watercress is not available. Watercress is a mild acid that is useful as a scalp tonic and hair cleanser, and because of its high zinc and biotin levels, it has been used in tonic form as a natural remedy for thinning hair.

Hydroponic crop

Wild watercress growing in a stream

⚠ **WARNING!**
Care must be taken if watercress is grown in proximity to animal pastures because of the risk of contamination with liver fluke parasites found in manure. Cooking renders the watercress safe.

Triticum aestivum

WHEATGRASS

The narrow, bright green blades of wheatgrass are actually the first tender leaves of the *Triticum aestivum*, or common wheat, seedling. Wheatgrass is available in health stores and specialty grocery stores, usually sold in shallow trays.

A HOME HARVEST

Wheatgrass is widely promoted for its nutritional properties and it is especially popular as a juice. Among its many reported health benefits is its positive impact on the digestive system and its potential to alleviate the symptoms of bowel disorders. As a juice, wheatgrass has a strong grassy flavor and aroma. It can be juiced on its own or combined with other fruits and vegetables. It is also available in powdered form. Wheatgrass is easily grown at home, either in soil or hydroponically. It is suitable for small containers, as it can be harvested more than once; when each blade of grass divides, it is time to cut again, although the flavor and nutritional content deteriorate over time. It is a fast-growing food, maturing from seed to harvest in nine or ten days.

Clockwise: sprouting wheatgrass; wheatgrass juice; harvesting wheatgrass

Achillea millefolium

YARROW

This clump-forming, flowering perennial is a native of the grasslands and pastures of North America. It is a familiar sight as a roadside weed, but the humble yarrow has many beneficial properties and a long history. The leaves and flowers are edible, and while it was a common food source up until the seventeenth century, wild yarrow is valued today primarily for its medicinal properties. Hardy and drought-tolerant, it also thrives in temperate regions of Europe and Asia.

Medicinal Uses

The many colorful common names for this plant, such as nosebleed plant, soldier's woundwort, stanchweed, and sanguinary, tell us something of the numerous medicinal properties of yarrow. Its use as a healing herb dates back centuries and it was particularly valued for its ability to stop bleeding. Its botanical name, *Achillea millefolium*, is derived from the Greek mythological figure Achilles, who according to legend carried yarrow into battle to staunch the wounds of his soldiers (another name for yarrow is *militaris*). Yarrow was also an important healing plant among the Native American peoples, who made use of the leaves, blossoms, stalks, and roots to reduce fever, alleviate pain, and aid sleep.

CHAPTER 2

FRUITS & BERRIES

Persea americana

AVOCADO

The avocado tree is native to Mexico and Central America, and its fruit is consumed around the world. Avocado trees vary in characteristic and habit; avocado fruits are classified into three types—Mexican, Guatemalan, and West Indian—according to their respective climates.

AVOCADO VARIETIES

Often referred to as the "avocado pear," the edible part of the avocado is actually a berry containing a single large seed. It is also known as "alligator pear" because of its warty skin. The most common commercially available type of avocado is the dark-skinned Hass variety, but there are many other cultivars grown worldwide, including the smooth, green-skinned type, and a new South African giant variety, Avozilla, which measures over seven inches in length and three pounds in weight.

Avocados growing on a tree

Large single avocado seed

Culinary Uses

Avocados were a staple food of the Aztecs— the name "avocado" is derived from the Aztec word *āhuacatl*. The Aztecs prepared the food as a mashed sauce similar to the popular guacamole of today. Beloved of college students and a familiar sight at barbecues and cocktail parties, guacamole is a healthy, easy-to-prepare dish. There are many minor variations and personal preferences for this dish, but in essence it comprises mashed, ripe avocados combined with salt, onion, garlic, tomatoes, chili, and lime juice, generally served with tortilla chips. Compared to other fruits, avocados have a very high fat content. More than half of this fat is the "good" monounsaturated fat, which can help to lower cholesterol and reduce the risk of heart attack.

Guacamole and tortilla chips

Capsicum annuum

BELL PEPPER

Bell peppers belong to the *Capsicum* genus, which contains many species of peppers, ranging from the mild-flavored bell pepper (or sweet pepper) to the spiciest chili pepper. The fruits can be categorized into three broad types: sweet (mild), chili (hot), and ornamental.

RED, AMBER, GREEN

The bell pepper most commonly available in the United States comes in two forms: green, which is the fruit in its unripe state (and consequently slightly bitter tasting); and red, orange, and yellow, which are the same as the green pepper but in a ripened state (these are also sweeter-tasting). Other varieties bear fruits that are purple, brown, and white, and the species varies enormously in terms of shape, size, color, and taste.

Green pepper ripening

Culinary Uses

The large interior cavity and firm flesh of the bell pepper make it a natural receptacle for other foods. Recipes for stuffed peppers are found wherever bell peppers are cultivated, and it seems no two recipes are alike. Each recipe, though, begins with a raw bell pepper. The pepper is washed, the top quarter sliced off and set aside, and the pepper is deseeded. A savory mixture of meat, seafood, vegetables (or all of the above) combined with herbs and spices is spooned into the cavity, capped with the bell pepper "lid," placed upright onto a baking tray, and roasted in the oven until the flesh is tender.

Capsicum annuum
Chili Pepper

THE SCOVILLE SCALE

The Scoville scale is a system for measuring the heat factor of spicy foods, including chili peppers. Units on the scale correspond to the amount of capsaicin—a natural chemical that produces a sensation of heat—present in the plant. The more concentrated the capsaicin, the hotter the heat factor will be, and consequently the pepper will rank higher level on the Scoville scale.

SCOVILLE HEAT UNIT EXAMPLES

15,000,000–16,000,000	Pure capsaicin
8,600,000–9,100,000	Various capsaicinoids
5,000,000–5,300,000	Law enforcement–grade pepper spray
855,000–1,359,000	Infinity Chili, Naga Viper pepper, bhut jolokia
350,000–580,000	Red Savina habañero
100,000–350,000	Guntur chili, habañero chili, Scotch Bonnet, datil, rocoto, piri piri, Madame Jeanette
50,000–100,000	Bird's eye chili, malagueta pepper, pequin pepper
30,000–50,000	Cayenne pepper, ají dulce, tabasco pepper, cumari pepper
10,000–23,000	Serrano pepper, Peter pepper, Aleppo pepper
2,500–8,000	Jalapeño pepper, guajillo chili, New Mexico chili, paprika, Tabasco sauce
500–2,500	Anaheim pepper, poblano, rocotillo pepper, Peppadew, pardon pepper
100–500	Pimento, peperoncini, banana pepper

Clockwise: Habañero; Jalapeño; Bird's eye; Piri piri; Scotch Bonnet; Poblano

PEPPER GALLERY

Thousands of pepper cultivars are produced worldwide, ranging in flavor from mildly sweet to fiery hot and coming in a wide variety of colors and shapes.

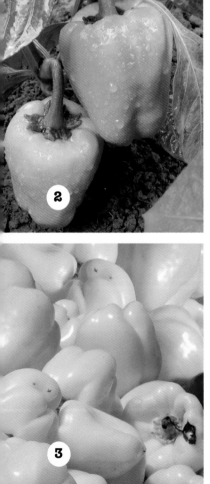

1: Red, yellow, and orange bell peppers;
2: Orange bell peppers; 3: Yellow bell
peppers; 4: Purple bell peppers; 5: Red bell
peppers; 6: Mix of bell and chili peppers

Momordica charantia

BITTER MELON

At first glance the leaves of *Momordica charantia* could be mistaken for grape vine. The bitter melon vine produces copious deeply lobed leaves, whose ragged edge gives the plant its name—*momordica* in Latin means "to bite." Bitter melon is a climbing vine widely grown in tropical and subtropical regions.

A BITTER PLEASURE

Bitter melon is prized in many Asian cuisines for the very quality that would make it unpalatable to most Western tastes. It is grown primarily for its edible fruits, but the leaves can also be consumed; all parts of the plant are extremely bitter in taste. This bitter element contributes interest and complexity to recipes. The fruits grow up to eight inches in length, and are harvested while they are still hard and green. If left on the vine to mature, the fruits will ripen to a bright yellow and eventually burst open to reveal bright red seed cases containing small black seeds.

Warty bitter melon fruits

Bitter melon on the vine

Medicinal Uses

In Asia, South America, India, and East Africa, bitter melon has long been used as traditional medicine to treat the symptoms of illnesses ranging from the common cold and digestive complaints to kidney stones. The bitterness of the fruit is due in part to high levels of quinine, useful in the treatment of malaria. It also possesses a natural hypoglycemic action, which has been shown to lower blood sugar levels. This makes it a valuable plant in modern pharmaceutical research and the search for effective treatments for type 2 diabetes.

Sliced bitter melon fruit

Ripe fruit bursting with seeds

Cucumis sativus

CUCUMBER

Cultivated since ancient times, there are hundreds of cucumber varieties available today. These fall into three broad categories: pickling, slicing, and the charmingly named "burpless" type. As these categories suggest, cucumbers are grown either for pickling or as a salad vegetable, and selected for their low gas-producing properties.

COOL, BUT NOT COLD

The cucumber plant is believed to have originated in India. It belongs to the Cucurbitaceae family and is a distant relative of the melon and pumpkin. The cucumber requires high temperatures to grow; in cooler northern climates these plants are generally grown inside a greenhouse or under a structure that can protect them from the cold.

Cold frames for warmth-loving plants

HOME SPA

The cucumber is not a nutrient-dense food; it is largely valued for its mild, refreshing flavor and crunchy texture. It has a high moisture content (topping out at a whopping 90%), anti-inflammatory properties, cucurbitacin, cucurmarin, and vitamins C and K, all of which help promote healthy skin.

Cucumber skin treatment

A cucumber slice over each eye is a traditional remedy for puffy eyes. The antioxidant properties in cucumber also help the skin retain moisture, and they can reduce wrinkles. Simply grating a cucumber and combining the strained liquid with rose water can make an easy home spa tonic.

Cucumis anguria

West Indian Gherkin

Like the cucumber, the West Indian gherkin is a climbing vine belonging to the same plant family. Its name is a little misleading; the plant originated in Africa, but is so-called because it was introduced into the United States from Jamaica. It is also known as burr gherkin for its prickly, round fruits. Its flavor is similar to that of cucumber, and it is prepared in much the same ways, although the West Indian gherkin is also consumed as a cooked vegetable and is especially popular as such in Brazil.

Prickly fruit of the West Indian gherkin

Solanum melongena

EGGPLANT

The fruit of *Solanum melongena* is known by many different names around the world. The French call it aubergine, the Italians call it *melenzana*, in parts of Asia and South Africa it is called *brinjal*, and its Hindi name is *baigan*. Known in the United States as eggplant, its name is derived from pre-nineteenth–century white cultivars, which were similar in size and shape to a swan's egg.

Rare white eggplants

THE KING OF VEGETABLES

The deep purple color and glossy skin of the eggplant make it one of the most beautiful vegetables. In India it is often referred to as the "king of vegetables." Eggplants can taste slightly bitter, especially as they increase in size, but the fleshy meat acts like a sponge and carries other flavors in stews and casseroles. Sprinkling slices of raw eggplant with salt and rinsing before cooking can help reduce bitterness. Eggplants have been produced in a number of varieties. In addition to the commonly available purple/black type, Sicilian or "graffiti" eggplant has streaked skin; Indian eggplant is short and round; and Japanese eggplant is long and thin, with lighter purple skin.

Sicilian eggplants

Eggplant flower

Culinary Uses

A popular Punjabi dish is *baigan bartha,* an aromatic curry made with roasted eggplant. Despite the complexity of its flavors and the many spices it contains, it is a simple dish to prepare. Eggplant is roasted until tender, then the flesh is scooped out and combined with chopped onion, ginger, garlic, and tomatoes. The spices cayenne, curry, asafoetida powder, and garam masala are added to the mix, along with cumin and mustard seeds that have been popped over heat. The dish is garnished with cilantro and served with parathas, naan, or rotis breads.

Baigan bartha *(roasted eggplant)*

Coccinia grandis

IVY GOURD

Coccinia grandis, or ivy gourd, has a number of colorful names—not least of which is "gentleman's toes"—but the common name, baby watermelon, perhaps best sums up the appearance of the plant.

Flowering ivy gourd

A MIXED BLESSING

While being immune to most pests and diseases, in many countries *Coccinia grandis* is considered a serious pest itself, and it is listed on the Global Invasive Species Database as a noxious weed. It is a tropical vine, a fast-growing, aggressive perennial that can quickly overtake trees and shrubs and smother them, while forming a dense canopy. It also has an extensive root system, making it extremely challenging to eradicate. Its geographic range is wide, spreading from Africa and Asia to Australia and North America. Despite its notoriety, in other countries ivy gourd is enjoyed as a food and appreciated for its ornamental features.

Ripe ivy gourd fruits

Sliced immature green fruits

Culinary Uses

In India ivy gourd is known as *tindora* and it is a beloved vegetable. The ripe fruit is bright red and soft, and can be eaten raw or added to soups and stews. In its unripe green form the fruit resembles small cucumbers; it is firm and slightly bitter tasting. This forms the basis for the traditional Gujurati dish tindora and potato curry, a piquant dish that combines green ivy gourd and potato, flavored with cumin and mustard seeds, and seasoned with Indian spices. The dish is finished with yogurt, garnished with cilantro, and served with *parathas* (Indian bread).

Tindora and potato curry

GOURD GALLERY

Pumpkin and other winter squash are part of a large botanical family that contains both edible and ornamental gourds.

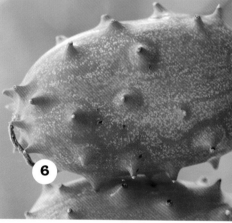

1: Mixed daisy gourds; 2: Spiny bitter gourd; 3: Ornamental crookneck squash; 4: Flat and heirloom pumpkin; 5: Bottle gourd; 6: Horned melon; 7: West Indian gherkin

Olea europaea

OLIVE

Olea europaea is one of the oldest known cultivated trees. Its history predates written language, but historians believe it was first cultivated for its fruit some 6,000 years ago. The olive tree is native to Asia Minor and can be found throughout the Mediterranean and North Africa.

A LATE BLOOMER

The olive tree is instantly recognizable for its rounded shape and spreading form—which rarely exceeds 40 feet in height. It has attractive silver-gray foliage and gnarled trunks, and is grown both for its edible fruit and for the valuable oil made from the pressed fruit. It is a slow-growing tree and will not produce fruit until it is at least five years old, but a single olive tree can live and continue to bear fruit for over 1,000 years.

1,000-year-old olive trees growing on the Adriatic coast

Olives on the branch

Extra virgin olive oil

ATHLETE'S HONOR

The olive was first cultivated in Greece and it played an important role in the country's economic development. The Greek goddess Athena is attributed with bringing the olive to Greece. Athena and the sea god Poseidon competed against each other for patronage of the city. Poseidon brought forth salt water, which was not of much use to the people; Athena struck her staff in the ground and created the olive tree. The olive is closely associated with ancient Olympic games held in honor of Athena's father, Zeus. First records of the games date to 776 BC in the Peloponnesus in the southern part of Greece. Winning athletes were crowned with a *kotinos*, a wreath made from olive branches woven into a headdress.

Olive branch Olympic crown

Cucurbita pepo

PUMPKIN

The pumpkin originated in the Americas. It belongs to the Cucurbitaceae, or gourd family, which contains many species, both edible and nonedible. Pumpkins can grow to be extremely large, weighing up to 100 pounds.

A HALLOWEEN TRADITION

In the United States the pumpkin is synonymous with Halloween, when it is used as a holiday decoration. The bright-orange outer skin of the pumpkin is tough enough to retain its shape even after being elaborately carved into a jack-o'-lantern. Traditionally a candle is lit inside the pumpkin at night, and it is set outside to illuminate gardens and pathways.

Halloween jack-o'-lantern

Culinary Uses

Pumpkin has a rich, slightly nutty flavor that lends itself well to many different kinds of soups and stews. It can also be consumed raw and is a nutritious vegetable high in vitamin A. One of the most popular ways to prepare this vegetable is as the sweet dessert pumpkin pie, a traditional Thanksgiving and winter holiday dish. A smaller, more delicately flavored "pie-pumpkin" is used to make this dish. The pumpkin flesh is cooked until soft, and the pulp is blended to a smooth consistency. This is combined with eggs, condensed milk, sugar, and spices, poured into a pastry pie base, and baked in the oven.

Pumpkin pie

Cucurbita maxima var. *turbaniformis*

Winter Squash

Unlike summer squash, which is harvested and eaten when young, these fruits are left on the vine until the skins have hardened. The tough outer rind of winter squash means that it can be stored through the winter months, as its name suggests. Winter squash come in a dazzling array of shapes, colors, and textures, and they are valued as much for their ornamental use as for their culinary use.

Turban squash

Cucurbita pepo ssp. *pepo*

SUMMER SQUASH

Summer squash is the name commonly used to describe the immature fruits of the *Cucurbito pepo* species, which includes pumpkins and other "hard" types of winter squash. Young, tender fruits are harvested early in the growing season before the skins become tough.

Zucchini in the garden

CONTAINER GARDENING

Summer squash is easy to grow from seed, but requires consistently warm temperatures throughout the growing season. Its trailing habit means that plants require considerable space in the garden, but compact varieties, such as dwarf-vine and bush varieties, may also be grown in large containers. It is a relatively high-yield species, producing eight to twelve pounds of fruit per plant.

Summer squash growing in a pot

Praecitrullus fistulosus
Tinda

As is the case with summer squash, tinda is harvested when the fruits are immature and the skins are still soft. Looking like a cross between a baby pumpkin and a green apple, tinda is part of the Cucurbitaceae family that includes the pumpkin. It is also known as Indian apple gourd. Tinda is a fast-growing annual vine cultivated in India, Pakistan, Afghanistan, and East Africa. It is a particularly popular vegetable in India (*tinda* is a Punjabi name). The whole fruit is eaten in curries and stews, and it is also pickled and candied. The seeds of the plant are edible as well; roasted seeds are eaten as a snack.

Harvested tinda

Solanum lycopersicum

TOMATO

The tomato is native to South America and historians estimate that it was cultivated as early as 500 BC. It was domesticated from the wild tomato—a small, hairy ancestor that bore little resemblance to the modern tomato. Today hundreds of varieties are available.

FRUIT OR VEGETABLE?

In 1883 in the United States the tomato was officially reclassified from its true botanical definition as a berry to a vegetable. A trade law introduced the same year imposed a 10 percent tax on all imported vegetables.

DEVIL'S FRUIT

Over the course of its long history the tomato has enjoyed a checkered reputation, being known as "poison apple," "devil's fruit," and "love apple." When it was first introduced to Europe from South America, the tomato was regarded with deep suspicion. In medieval Europe it was believed to be poisonous

Heirloom tomatoes

and was grown for ornamental use only (this is possibly due to its being related to deadly nightshade). The Italians were the first Europeans to begin incorporating tomatoes into their cuisine, in the seventeenth century. When it was no longer considered poisonous, the Catholic Church labeled it as sinful, believing it to inflame passions and incite lascivious behavior. The French took a slightly different view and regarded the tomato as an aphrodisiac.

The "love apple"

ICONIC AMERICAN PRODUCT

In 1897 Joseph Campbell patented a system for manufacturing condensed soup in a can, creating a cheap, mass-produced product that quickly became a staple in grocery stores nationwide. Tomato was the inaugural flavor. In 1962 the pop artist Andy Warhol elevated this humble product to iconic status in his *Campbell's Soup Cans* series, replicating the way the 32 flavors of Campbell's soups were displayed on shelves in grocery stores.

Campbell's tomato soup can

Physalis philadelphica

TOMATILLO

A small, husk-covered berry, the tomatillo is central to Mexican cuisine. It was cultivated in pre-Columbian times, and it continues to be an important Mexican crop today.

GREEN WHEN RIPE

The diminutive tomatillo looks like a small tomato encased in a papery husk, but the tomatillo is considered ripe when the husk splits open and the fruit is still green. Other names for it are Mexican green tomato and husk tomato. Although they are typically green, there are also yellow and purple heirloom varieties. Tomatillo belongs to the Solanaceae, or nightshade family, which includes potatoes, tomatoes, and eggplant, and it is the same genus as the ornamental plant *Physalis alkekengi*, or Chinese lantern.

Ripe green and purple varieties of tomatillo

Ornamental Chinese lantern

Culinary Uses

Tomatillos are used in many Mexican dishes, both raw and cooked. Although similar in appearance to a green tomato, the flavor of a tomatillo is different; it is tangy and slightly sour. Perhaps the most popular use of the tomatillo is in the traditional Mexican preparation *salsa verde*, or green salsa, which combines roasted or boiled tomatillos with raw onion, jalapeño, garlic, cilantro, and lime juice. Salsa verde can be served in a number of ways: as a sauce for meats, as a dip with tortilla chips, and as a piquant flavoring used to enhance other dishes.

Salsa verde

TOMATO GALLERY

The tomato is one of the most extensively grown vegetables in the United States; thousands of cultivars exist, including many popular heirloom varieties.

1: Ribbed tomato; 2: Golden red and yellow marbled heirloom; 3: Yellow plum tomato; 4: Mixed Kumato and Campari cultivars; 5: Heirloom tomatoes; 6: Mixed tomato varieties; 7: Purple cultivar

Vanilla planifolia

VANILLA

Vanilla is native to Mexico and was cultivated by the Totonac and Aztec peoples long before the Spanish conquistadors brought it to Europe in the sixteenth century. It is the only edible fruit of a species of climbing orchid belonging to the Orchidaceae family.

Melipona bee

Vanilla orchid flower

Vanilla orchid vine climbing a host tree

Immature vanilla pods on the vine

A RAPID CLIMBER

Also known as flat-leafed vanilla, the vanilla orchid is a tropical vine with thick, fleshy leaves. It produces slender, daffodil-like flowers that develop into long thin pods containing black seeds. Green, unripe pods on the vine have no scent or flavor; those attributes develop as the pod is dried and chemical compounds in the pod crystalize. In its native habitat the vanilla vine has adapted to climb up trees, attaching by means of aerial roots. Two main species of orchid are grown for their vanilla pods—*Vanilla planifolia* and *Vanilla pompon*.

STANDING IN FOR THE BEES

Initial attempts to cultivate vanilla beyond its native environment failed because the plant depended entirely on the native Melipona bee for pollination. This little bee is found only in Mexico. Eventually Edmond Albius discovered a system for hand-pollinating the plants. He was the twelve-year-old son of a slave working on a plantation in Réunion, a colonial French island in the Indian Ocean. His discovery revolutionized vanilla production. Vanilla flowers are hand-pollinated to this day, making it a labor-intensive and expensive product. The flower of the vanilla orchid opens for just twenty-four hours; in order to produce, pods must be pollinated within the first eight to twelve hours. The plant is also slow to mature, and it can take up to five years before it bears fruit.

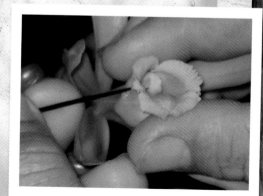
Hand-pollinating a vanilla orchid flower

Benincasa hispida

WINTER MELON

This annual vine gets its name from the waxy coating that develops on the mature fruit, which makes it possible to store the plant through the winter. The flesh is not sweet, as its name might suggest, but it has a mild flavor similar to summer squash, and is eaten as a savory vegetable.

GROWING WINTER MELON

Winter melon originated in Southeast Asia, and it is widely eaten throughout Asia. This annual plant is easy to grow from seed, but it requires very warm weather to thrive. The fruits grow to a great size, and they can easily weigh up to 40 pounds. It is a climbing plant, but because of its heavy fruits the plant is often grown on the ground; with additional support it can also be grown on trellises. The plant is self-fertile, bearing male and female flowers. The flowers, leaves, seeds, and fruit are all edible.

Young winter melon fruit

Culinary Uses

The skin of young winter melon fruits have a hairy fuzz, but the outer coating of mature fruits are smooth and waxy, and firm enough to be used as bowls for the traditional Chinese dish *dong gwa jong*, or winter melon soup. In the same way a Halloween pumpkin is hollowed out, the seeds and fibrous inner part of the fruit are scooped out and discarded. A layer of flesh is also removed, leaving a thick wall of flesh inside the tough outer skin. The removed flesh is diced, combined with meats or seafood and stock, and returned to the hollowed-out bowl. Then the whole thing is steamed until tender. The flesh of the bowl absorbs the flavors of the soup, and everything is eaten so that all that remains is the tough outer skin. In Chinese banquets the bowls are brought to the table intricately carved with traditional motifs like dragons or the phoenix, and lettering.

Edible winter melon bowl and soup

Winter melon on the vine

CHAPTER 3

PODDED VEGETABLES

Vigna angularis

ADZUKI BEAN

The small, red adzuki bean is a genus of flowering legume native to China and Japan, where it is the second most important pulse crop. It is also known as azuki bean, aduki bean, and *chi dou*.

Profusely seeded adzuki bean pods

Adzuki beans with distinctive hilum

JAPANESE KING OF BEAN

Adzuki, or red bean, is an important East Asian food appearing in many preparations in Japanese and Chinese cuisines. Adzuki beans are usually consumed in their dried form. The mature beans are soaked and boiled before being puréed as red bean paste or used as flour; however, young green pods and sprouts are also eaten. Adzuki beans are a low-fat, high-protein, high-fiber food, filled with beneficial antioxidants, minerals, and B vitamins. In addition, they are valued as one of the most easily digestible beans.

Red bean paste

Culinary Uses

In the West, legumes are mostly associated with savory dishes, but adzuki beans have a sweet, nutty flavor that makes them well suited to sweetened preparations, and they form the basis of many popular Asian confectionaries. Dessert is not a typical part of the Asian meal, but sweets are popular. Sweetened red bean paste is used as a filling for innumerable cakes, confectionaries, candies and ice cream. In 2009 an adzuki-flavored Pepsi cola was introduced to the Japanese market. Yokan is an elegant sweetened jelly made from flavored agar and either mixed or filled with red bean paste (much as a doughnut is filled with jelly). Great emphasis is placed on the appearance and presentation of these treats, which may be served after a meal or may accompany afternoon tea.

Elegant yokan *confectionary*

Apios americana

AMERICAN GROUNDNUT

The American groundnut is a perennial vinelike trailing plant belonging to the Fabaceae, or bean family. It is an indigenous wild food that can be found growing on forest floors and in thickets throughout the United States.

NUT OR NOT?

The American groundnut is not actually a nut at all. It produces edible beans and long, thin underground stems that develop around tuberous swellings along their length. These swellings constitute the groundnut. It is a high-energy, starchy vegetable similar in taste to the potato, but it contains three times as much protein. The plant is recognizable for its pink, purple, or brownish-red flowers whose shape resembles conquistador helmets in miniature. Pinnate leaves grow in pairs along each stem.

Edible groundnut tubers

Distinctive groundnut flowers

Pinnate groundnut leaves

A THANKSGIVING FOOD

Other names for the American groundnut suggest its historic importance as a food source; it is also known as the potato bean and the Indian potato. American groundnuts were a staple of Native American peoples, and it can still be found growing in historic Native American sites. It was also a valuable source of protein for the first Pilgrim settlers, who were taught how to find and prepare the vegetable by the indigenous peoples. The plant produces groundnuts year-round, making it an invaluable source of nutrition during the winter. To prepare for eating the groundnuts were first peeled, then boiled, roasted, or dried and ground into a powder, and sometimes preserved in maple syrup.

 WARNING! American groundnuts often grow alongside poison ivy, so great care must be taken in foraging this plant.

"Leaves of three, let it be!" Poison ivy leaves in distinctive triplet form

Vigna unguiculata ssp. *unguiculata*

BLACK-EYED PEA

Ripe black-eyed pea pods

This bean takes its name from the distinctive black spot surrounding the raised hilum, or seed scar. The black-eyed pea, or bean, is a subspecies of the cowpea, and is one of the most important and widely cultivated food crops worldwide. It is grown for its high-protein beans, which are added to recipes after soaking or boiling. Its edible leaves and shoots are also highly nutritious.

A GOOD-LUCK FOOD

The black-eyed pea is heat- and drought-tolerant, and thrives in semiarid and tropical climates. Believed to have been first cultivated in Africa, it was introduced to the U.S. early in the seventeenth century. In the United States the black-eyed

Dried black-eyed peas

pea is cultivated mainly in the South, where it plays an important role in traditional Southern cuisine. In the South it is considered lucky to eat black-eyed peas on New Year's Day. Pink- or purple-eyed peas are also commonly available and marketed as dried, frozen, or canned beans.

"Hoppin' John" a traditional Southern dish

Vigna unguiculata ssp. sesquipedalis

Yardlong Bean

This extraordinary bean grows not to a yard in length, as its name suggests, but on average to 18 inches. The yardlong bean, also known as asparagus bean and Chinese long bean, is a close relative of the black-eyed pea. It is a vigorous climbing vine, cultivated for its edible green pods, which are harvested before the seeds mature and while the pods are still tender.

This vegetable is widely grown in Southeast Asia and China, where it is prized for its crisp, flavorful pods. In the United States it is available largely in Asian and specialty grocery stores.

Green and purple varieties of yardlong beans

Cicer arietinum

CHICKPEA

The chickpea is one of the top three pulses consumed worldwide, and it is a vital source of protein for large populations living in drought-prone parts of Asia and Africa.

AN ANCIENT SOURCE

Cicer arietinum is one of the earliest known cultivated plants; fossilized remains have been found dating as early as 3500 BC. The biggest producer of chickpeas today is India, where it is known as *chana*. Several types of *Cicer arietinum* exist with minor differences depending on region.

Chickpeas develop inside light green fuzzy pods, usually containing two or three peas each. The foliage is silvery-green and delicate, with slightly fuzzy stems. The flowers of the plant are white, pink, or purple and similar in form to the pea plant.

Fuzzy chickpea pods

Bowl of chickpeas

Culinary Uses

The chickpea is most commonly associated with Middle Eastern cuisine, especially when prepared as hummus, the creamy savory dish of ground chickpeas and sesame seeds. Other popular chickpea dishes around the world are:

Falafel, fried chickpea balls served with tahini sauce

Cocido Madrileño, a hearty traditional Spanish stew from Madrid

Channa Masala, a richly spiced Indian curry of chickpeas, onions, and tomatoes

Eetli Nohut, a Turkish beef stew with chickpeas, onions, and spices, served with rice pilaf and pickles

Chana dal Halwa, a traditional Indian dessert made from ground chickpeas, almonds, cashews, and pistachios mixed with eggs, sugar, and ghee

Falafel with tahini sauce

Cajanus cajan

Pigeon Pea

The pigeon pea belongs to the same family of beans and legumes as the peanut and the chickpea. It is a drought-tolerant woody shrub native to Asia and Africa, and is cultivated throughout the tropics and subtropics for its edible pealike seeds. The seeds, known as pigeon peas, grow inside edible seedpods. Pigeon peas are a high-protein pulse, making them an important food source among vegetarian populations. The leaves, flowers, and seeds are also widely used in traditional medicines.

Dried pigeon peas

Vicia faba

FAVA BEAN

The fava bean is a historically important plant of great lineage, and it was a staple food of ancient civilizations. It is an upright, hardy annual believed to have originated in the Mediterranean and North Africa. Today the fava bean is cultivated worldwide. Other common names for this bean are broad bean, Windsor bean, field bean, Scotch bean, and horse bean.

TOUGH EXTERIOR, TENDER HEART

Vicia faba is grown primarily for its highly nutritious beans. There are three types of culinary varieties, which produce small, medium, or large beans. The immature bean, or seed, may be eaten as a fresh vegetable. Fresh fava beans have a tough outer skin that most people prefer to remove before eating. This can be time-consuming, but cooking the beans, then cooling them quickly in cold water, will allow the skins to slip off easily. The plant produces striking black-and-white flowers that are highly fragrant and will attract pollinating bees. It is fast-growing, and the seeds are variable in color. The thick, leathery pods are green when young, and they darken to brown or black when mature. Mature seeds are used as dried beans have a long storage

Podded fava seeds

Dried fava beans

and life.

Distinctive fava bean flowers

Culinary Uses

Fava beans are the main ingredient of a classic Middle Eastern breakfast dish, *ful maddamas*. This is a comfort food made with boiled fava beans mixed with tahini sauce and seasoned with cumin, lemon, salt, and garlic. Ful maddamas is generally served with pita bread.

Ful maddamas

Phaseolus vulgaris

GREEN BEAN

Green beans belong to the Fabaceae family, a large, diverse botanical family of legumes that are grown for their immature pods to be eaten as a green vegetable, or are harvested for their dried seeds such as kidney beans, black beans, navy beans, and many others.

HEALTHY CONVENIENCE FOOD

A great favorite in the United States, green beans are also known as string beans and snap beans, and they are popular as a fresh, frozen, or canned vegetable. They have a long shelf life

Some green beans have a vigorous climbing habit

and can be stored in the refrigerator for several days without losing freshness or nutrients. There are more than 130 green bean cultivars available today. Plants come in two main types: compact bush form or pole (climbing) form.

GREEN BEANS FOR A LONG LIFE

Green beans are high in antioxidants and the vitamins K, C, and A. They also contain three carotenoids: beta-carotene, lutein, and zeaxanthin, all of which are important for maintaining healthy eyes. Vitamin K is essential for healthy bones and helps to prevent bone density loss; it is also vital for healthy cartilage and connective tissue. Vitamin C boosts the immune system, lowers cholesterol, and helps to regulate high blood pressure. Green beans are also high in vitamin A, which, in addition to its cancer-fighting properties, helps to preserve smooth, healthy skin.

Clockwise: red string beans; green beans; yellow wax beans; purple beans; dragon tongue beans

Cyamopsis tetragonoloba

GUAR

Guar is grown primarily in India and Pakistan, where it is valued both as an edible plant and for the natural thickening properties of its seeds.

Guar pods

CLIMATE CONDITIONS

Guar is a drought-tolerant annual legume that thrives in semiarid climates. India leads in the production of guar, and guar's unique properties are in part due to the Indian climate, which provides both arid and monsoon weather patterns. The leaves and young, tender pods of the plant are used in stews and salads.

INDUSTRIAL GUAR

Grinding dried guar seeds results in a water-soluble, odorless powder, which is exported all over the globe as a binding and stabilizing agent. Guar gum is found in a wide range of foods, including ice cream, and it is often used in gluten-free products as a substitute for wheat. Guar gum also has significant industrial applications in the manufacture of cosmetics, paper products, textiles, fire retardants, and even explosives. In recent years it has become a valuable resource for the oil industry, specifically in the hydraulic fracturing process. Guar is now grown in certain parts of the United States.

Guar is a common stabilizer in many foods

Lathyrus sativus

INDIAN PEA

Indian pea is a drought-tolerant plant in the Fabaceae, or legume family. It is thought to have originated in the Balkans, but it has naturalized in large parts of the Mediterranean and the Middle East.

FRESH OR DRIED

Other common names for the Indian pea are grass pea, chickling pea, dogtooth pea, and white pea. Immature tender peas can be eaten as a green vegetable. In some places, whole pods are boiled and salted, and then sold as snacks. Mature seeds are hard and require soaking for at least 24 hours before cooking. Dried seeds are used in stews and casseroles, or are ground to make flours and pastes.

SAFE IN MODERATION

The pretty flowers of the edible Indian pea range from vivid blue to red, purple, pink, and white. They are very similar in appearance to the ornamental sweet pea (*Lathyrus odoratus*), which is poisonous. The seeds of the edible Indian pea contain a toxic amino acid that is safe to eat in small amounts; however, a steady diet of these can lead to the development of a serious neurological disease called lathyrism, which causes paralysis. Historically, incidences of lathyrism increase during times of drought and famine when other crops fail and people are forced to rely on the Indian Pea as their sole source of food.

Drought-resistant pea pods

Dried, split Indian peas

Lens culinaris

LENTIL

Lens culinaris is an annual herbaceous legume grown for its high-protein seeds, which are consumed all over the world. Lentils were one of the earliest foods to be cultivated, sometime between 7,000 and 5,000 BC in the Fertile Crescent, a geographic semicircle that extends from northeastern Africa to the Persian Gulf.

COLORFUL VARIETIES

There are many named varieties of lentils that vary slightly in terms of their nutritional content or growing habit. The most common variety in the United States is the brown lentil. Other varieties include yellow, red, black, and green lentils, and the smaller French green variety, *lentilles du puy*.

Lentil plant in flower

A FAMILIAR FORM

Lentils are important to Mediterranean, Middle Eastern, and Indian cuisines. The young, tender pods of the plant can be eaten as a green vegetable, but the seeds are generally cooked in stews and casseroles, or they are dried and ground into flour to make breads. The modern word for a scientific lens is a seventeenth-century derivation of the Latin word for lentil, *lens*; the name was adopted because of the similarity in shape and form between a split lentil and a lens.

Scientific lens

Convex form of split lentils

Phaseolus lunatus

LIMA BEAN

Lima beans are large, edible seeds of the climbing legume *Phaseolus lunatus*, native to Central and South America. It is believed to have been first cultivated in Peru about 4,000 years ago.

A NUTRITIOUS STAPLE

The lima bean plant bears prolific protein-rich seeds, or beans, and thrives in tropical and subtropical climates, making it an important food crop in parts of Africa. Known also as butter beans, lima beans are valued for their mild, buttery flavor, and they appear in cuisines around the world. Immature lima beans can be cooked and eaten as a fresh vegetable, or they can

Peruvian Moche pottery with bean motif, c. 500 BC

Lima bean vine

be allowed to mature on the vine, and then harvested for use as a dried bean. Dried beans are soaked before cooking and used in soups and stews, or are ground and used as a flour.

Immature lima bean pod

Dried lima beans

Culinary Uses

Lima beans are a main ingredient of succotash, an inexpensive but nutritionally complete meal that was popular in the United States during the Great Depression. Records for this simple dish date back as far as 1751, after Native Americans first introduced the recipe to Pilgrim settlers. The name "succotash" is believed to derive from the Algonquin Native American word for broken corn, *misquatash*. Succotash endures today as a traditional Thanksgiving food in the Northeast and some states in the South. Historically the dish combined kernels of corn with dried peas and some form of wild meat or animal fat. Lima beans eventually became the standard bean for the dish, and ham the preferred meat, cooked with butter and a light cream sauce. There are, however, many regional variations.

Traditional succotash dish

WARNING!
Lima beans should not be eaten raw, as they contain high levels of cyanogenic glycosides. Soaking and boiling the beans (in an open pan) will destroy the toxins.

Lupinus albus

LUPINI

Of the varieties of edible lupine, the Mediterranean white lupine (L. albus) and the more colorful Andean lupine (L. mutabilis) have the longest histories as food. Lupines are a flowering genus of the Fabaceae, or legume family. The plants produce fuzzy pods containing nutritious, beanlike seeds. To the Incas these were a staple food known as tarwi; in Europe lupinis are popular as a snack food.

Heavily seeded lupine pods

COTTAGE GARDEN FLOWER

In North America lupines are grown primarily for their ornamental value in the garden. The lupine is an easy-to-grow, drought-tolerant perennial that thrives in poor soil. This plant has the added advantage of being able to take up nitrogen from the air and improve the quality of the soil, which makes them good companion plants in both flower and vegetable gardens. Lupines produce tall flower spikes above attractive silver-gray leaves. Their height and showy flowers make them an excellent backdrop for other plants, and they can grow happily against a wall or on steeply

Lupines in the garden

sloped or graveled areas. There are numerous colorful varieties including rainbow hybrid, but the ancient blue strain is the hardiest. Not all lupines produce edible seeds.

Rainbow lupine and other colorful lupine cultivars

Culinary Uses

Lupini beans must be soaked for at least 24 hours, boiled, and then rinsed repeatedly before eating. This is necessary to remove bitter-tasting, toxic alkaloids that are also dangerous if eaten in large quantities. Presoaked, ready-to-eat lupinis can be purchased pickled in brine or vacuum-packed. In Italy lupinis served with olives is a traditional dish eaten on feast days. The nutty flavor and firm texture of the beans complements the saltiness of the olives. The beans are served in their skins; to eat, a bean is held in the fingers, the tough outer skin gently torn open with the teeth, and the inner part of the bean squeezed into the mouth.

Lupinis ready to eat

Vigna aconitifolia

MOTH BEAN

The name *moth bean* (pronounced "mote") is derived from a Hindi word and is not associated with the insect. The plant is a highly drought-tolerant legume native to India and Pakistan, where it is known as matki bean. Other names for the bean are mat bean, mother bean, and dew gram.

Low-growing moth bean vine

LIVING MULCH

The moth bean plant withstands very hot climates—up to 120°F—making it an invaluable crop plant in areas prone to drought. It is cultivated primarily in India, but also in other hot, dry regions around the world. It has a low, mat-forming habit, and is useful as a dense ground cover that will smother weeds, retain moisture, and combat soil erosion. It also improves the soil by fixing nitrogen. In India the plant is grown for its edible green pods and tiny seeds, or beans, which measure only 3–4 mm. The split beans are typically used to make dahl; the fresh green peas, shoots, and pods are also eaten as green vegetables. Moth beans can be sprouted and used in salads or fried in oil and served as a crunchy snack as well.

Tiny moth beans

Vigna radiata

MUNG BEAN

Vigna radiata, or mung bean, is a nutrient-dense legume grown for its fresh bean sprouts or dried beans. The round, green seeds are an easy-to-digest, high-protein food popular throughout Asia. Like the red adzuki bean, dried mung beans have a vast range of culinary applications in both sweet and savory dishes.

Flowering mung bean plant

Sprouted mung beans

SKIN-DEEP BENEFITS

Sometimes called green pea flour or green bean starch, mung bean flour is a fine-grained starch used to make glass noodles, pastas, dumplings, and a variety of pastries and confectionaries. It is gluten-free and an excellent alternative to wheat flour. Mung bean flour is also used as a popular natural facial treatment in Asia. The flour is available in the United States, but can easily be made at home by grinding dried mung beans. To make a gentle, chemical-free exfoliating face pack, simply mix finely ground mung bean flour with a little lukewarm water (and one or two drops of your favorite essential oil, if desired) and apply the paste to the face for ten minutes. Gently massage the face before rinsing off with warm water.

Dried and ground mung beans

Abelmoschus esculentus

OKRA

Known in the southern United States as gumbo, the British name for this vegetable, "lady's fingers," perhaps best describes its slender, tapered form.

FLOWERING BEAUTY

Okra is a fast-growing, high-yield plant native to Africa. It is widely cultivated in the Middle East, India, Africa, and in southern parts of the United States. It belongs to the Malvaceae family and is related to the flowering plants mallow, hibiscus, and hollyhock, whose blossoms are somewhat similar in appearance. Okra flowers can be used in floral arrangements, and dried fruits are also valued for their ornamental interest.

Harvested okra

Culinary Uses

For many, okra is a one of life's pleasures, but for others it can be an acquired taste. The slightly hairy pods must be harvested while still young; there is a relatively small window of time before they become woody and coarse. This, and the plant's mucilaginous property, which creates a slimy texture when cooked, can be unattractive. To counter sliminess the vegetable must be either cooked very briefly, as in stir-fried dishes, or cooked for a long time until the sliminess is reduced. Gumbo, a traditional dish of the Deep South, falls into the latter category. There are many variations on the gumbo dish depending on location and tradition, but all gumbos start with a roux to which the so-called Cajun trinity of vegetables is added: bell pepper, onion, and celery. Okra is also added to the mix, and it acts as a natural thickener. The ingredients are consolidated with stock, spicy seasonings, and combinations of meat and seafood, and then simmered to a desirable consistency.

Pork gumbo

Chopped okra

Dried okra fruits

Pisum sativum

PEAS

The common garden, field, or English pea is an herbaceous vine belonging to the Fabaceae family. Hundreds of forms have been developed, broadly grouped into those grown for green immature peas; for mature dried peas; and those grown for tender whole pods (sugar snap peas and snow peas). The word *pea* refers to the spherical podded seed of the plant in its immature green stage, or mature dried stage.

GREEN PEA: A RELATIVE NEWCOMER
The pea was first domesticated in Southwest Asia around 3,000 years ago, but archeological finds date it to the Neolithic Middle East. Dried peas were eaten long before green peas became popular in seventeenth-century Europe. The ancient Romans

Pea pods on the vine

Pea flowers

believed peas in their green state were poisonous. Today peas are widely cultivated around the globe, and more than half of the production ends up canned or frozen. The common pea is easy to grow in the garden. It is a cool-season plant tolerant of slight frosts, so planting it early ensures the biggest harvest. Production slows to a halt when hot summer weather kicks in.

Harvested fresh peas

Yellow split peas

Culinary Uses

Dried peas are at the heart of a traditional savory dish dating back to medieval England. Pease porridge (also known as pease pudding) is made from yellow split peas that have been soaked overnight and boiled for at least an hour with onion, carrot, and bay leaves. The mixture is puréed to a smooth consistency, seasoned with salt, pepper, and a little vinegar, and traditionally served with boiled ham and bread. The nursery rhyme and clapping game associated with this dish also gives cautionary advice as to its shelf life:

Pease porridge hot,
Pease porridge cold,
Pease porridge in the pot,
Nine days old.

Traditional "Pease porridge" clapping game

Arachis hypogaea

PEANUT

The peanut is a legume native to South America, cultivated by the Incas and other pre-Columbian cultures. It is an annual herbaceous plant of the Fabaceae, or bean family. The peanuts develop in papery shells underground, and the entire plant must be dug up in order to harvest the crop.

Harvesting peanuts

AN AMERICAN CLASSIC

The peanut was introduced to the United States initially as livestock feed and became popular as a household food after the Civil War. Since then peanuts have become an integral part of American cuisine. Peanut butter entered the American market in 1904, when it was introduced at the St. Louis World's Fair. Just as soldiers in the Civil War had relied on peanuts as a source of protein, peanut butter was an important ration food for American soldiers in World Wars I and II. Today it is a fundamental part of the American diet.

Early American brand of canned peanut butter

Culinary Uses

Most people buy peanut butter in grocery stores, often having a lifelong loyalty to particular brands (and strong feelings about the relative merits of smooth or crunchy varieties). But peanut butter is an easy food to make at home, which can be a tastier, healthier option. All that is required is to grind fresh or roasted peanuts in a food processor until the consistency is smooth and creamy. Salt and sweeteners such as sugar, honey, maple syrup, or molasses can be added if desired.

Homemade peanut butter

Phaseolus coccineus

RUNNER BEAN

The runner bean is a fast-growing legume native to Central America. Other common names for the plant are scarlet runner bean and scarlet emperor bean, so called for its vivid red flowers. The plant also produces large, attractive kidney-shaped seeds in a variety of mottled colors ranging from pink, red, purple, and blue to glossy black.

Profuse scarlet flowers

HUMMINGBIRD ATTRACTOR

The profuse scarlet flowers produced by the runner bean plant attract butterflies and hummingbirds into the garden. In North America it is often grown only for its ornamental use, but runner beans are a favorite vegetable in Europe, where they are considered to be more flavorful than green beans. The whole pod is eaten, harvested while still young and tender. The long, blade-shaped pods are sliced diagonally, boiled or steamed, then served with a knob of butter. In Central America the thick, stocky roots are also eaten. The leaves of the runner plant are also edible, and the flowers make attractive edible garnishes for salads.

Hummingbird visiting runner bean flowers

Phaseolus acutifolius

Tepary Bean

The drought-tolerant tepary bean, from the same genus as runner beans, grows happily in arid and semidesert conditions. It is native to the southwestern United States and Mexico, where it was first cultivated in pre-Columbian times. It was a staple food for Native American peoples, and it is still widely grown in Mexico today. The plant bears long, fuzzy pods with small seeds that have a sweet, nutty flavor. The seeds are most often used in soups. The flowers are pink, lilac, lavender, or purple.

Tepary bean plant in flower

Ripe bean pods

DRIED PEAS & BEANS GALLERY

Legumes, or dried peas and beans, are a valuable source of protein, fiber, and vitamin B, adding color and texture to foods around the globe.

1: Painted Pony heirloom beans; 2: Black beans; 3: Black-eyed peas; 4: Puy green lentils; 5: Split Indian peas; 6: Kidney beans; 7: Runner beans; 8: Chickpeas

Pisum sativum var. *macrocarpon*

SNAP PEA

The snap (or sugar) pea is a cultivar of the common garden pea, but whereas garden peas are grown for their young seeds and shelled before eating, the crisp, edible pods of the snap pea are eaten whole.

TENDER PODS

The pod of the common garden pea has a fibrous inner membrane that contracts as it ripens, causing the pod to split open. Snap peas lack this inner membrane, so the pod remains tender and does not open when ripe. Like garden peas, snap peas are harvested while still young, when the pods are fat and round, but the seeds are not fully developed. Snap pea pods contain fewer peas—only three to five on average. Mature snap pea pods can develop a tough "string" running along the outer edge of the pod, which needs to be removed before eating.

Harvested snap peas

Stir-fried snap peas with sesame

Pisum sativum var. *saccharatum*

SNOW PEA

Like snap peas, the snow pea is a variety of common garden pea grown for its flat, edible pods, which are eaten whole. Unlike other peas, snow pea pods do not swell as they ripen. This variety is also commonly known by its French name, *mangetout* ("eat all").

A POPULAR HOME HARVEST

The snow pea is a cool-season plant; its name may derive from the fact that it can tolerate cold temperatures and light snow. The seeds can germinate in temperatures as low as 40°F. It is particularly popular in Asian cuisine, where it is used in stir-fried dishes together with the young leaves and "tips": young stems, shoots, and tendrils. Snow pea shoots are especially valued for their distinctive flavor, which is reminiscent of the pea, but grassy and delicate. The youngest, most tender shoots are best used in salads; older, firmer cuttings can be wilted in soups, or added at the last minute to stir- or flash-fried dishes. The snow pea is popular for home growing as it produces early, grows quickly, and is a "cut and come again" plant.

Clockwise: Snow pea "tips"; stir-fried dish with snow peas; fresh snow peas

Glycine max

SOYBEAN

The soybean is believed to have originated in East Asia, and it has been cultivated in China for 5,000 years. It did not arrive in the United States until the beginning of the nineteenth century. Today the U.S. leads global soybean production, followed by Brazil, Argentina, China, and India.

KING OF BEANS

Extremely rich in vegetable protein and the most easily digested legume, soybeans are an important food in its class. It has a great many culinary uses worldwide, but it is particularly important to East Asian cuisine. Soybeans are eaten in a mind-boggling variety of preparations. The seedlings are eaten in salads; raw green soybeans are boiled in their pods and salted (these are known by their Japanese name, *edamame*). Dried beans are ground with water to make soybean milk, and the milk is curdled to make tofu. Fermented kinds of soybean foods are soy sauce, miso, bean paste, and tempeh. Textured soy protein—a by-product of extracting soybean oil—is also used as a high-protein meat substitute.

Clockwise: block of tofu; textured soy protein; podded soybeans

Psophocarpus tetragonolobus

WINGED BEAN

Thought to have originated in East Africa, the winged bean is a vigorous tropical vine in the Fabaceae, or legume family, and is distinguishable by its frilly edged seedpods with lateral "fins." Other names for this plant are four-angled bean, asparagus pea, princess bean, goa bean, and dragon bean. Winged bean pods open when ripe, making a loud popping noise— the plant's botanical name contains the Greek word *psophocarpus*, meaning "noisy fruit."

A WIN-WIN PLANT

The winged bean is an exceptionally versatile plant both in culinary and agricultural terms. Every part of the plant is edible, from its roots to its flowers. It is disease-resistant, highly productive, and it thrives in hot, humid climates. It is also a highly nutritious vegetable: its leaves are high in protein, and they are an excellent source of vitamins A and C. The beans are rich

Winged beans on the vine

Distinctive pods

Sliced wing beans

in folates, minerals, and vitamins (including important B-complex vitamins). The roots are similar in flavor to sweet potato, but they are considerably higher in protein—20 percent compared to the average 7 percent protein count for similar tuberous vegetables.

MULTIPURPOSE VEGETABLE

The seeds of the winged bean are used in much the same way as soybeans, but they contain higher levels of protein. They can be processed as a milk or fermented to make a food similar to tempeh and tofu. They are also a rich source of edible oil. The immature seeds are eaten as green peas; the mature beans can be roasted and used as a coffee substitute. Young, tender pods are flavorful and similar in taste to green beans or asparagus, and the leaves are used as green potherbs. The large, attractive flowers and buds have a mushroomlike flavor. These can be eaten raw, steamed, or stir-fried, and they are also used to add color to rice and pastries. Not widely cultivated in the West, the winged bean features heavily in Indonesian, Malaysian, Vietnamese, and Cambodian cuisines.

Clockwise: winged bean pod and flower; purple winged beans; winged bean tubers; dried beans and seeds

CHAPTER 4

BULB & STEM VEGETABLES

Asparagus officinalis

ASPARAGUS

This delicately flavored herbaceous perennial is native to Europe, North Africa, and western Asia. Asparagus was cultivated in ancient times, and today it constitutes an important commercial crop. It is available in both green and white (i.e., blanched) forms. White asparagus is especially popular in Europe, where it is considered superior to green asparagus in both texture and flavor.

SLOW BUT SURE

There are numerous health and medicinal benefits associated with asparagus, but its primary use is as a culinary vegetable. The asparagus plant has feathery blue-green foliage and green or yellow bell-shaped flowers. Tender purple-tinged spears are harvested early in spring just as the shoots emerge from the ground, before the buds and scalelike leaves along the spear have unfurled or "ferned out." Asparagus is slow to mature, and plants grown from seed will not produce a significant harvest for at least four years; growing the plant from a crown will shorten this process by one year. On the other hand, asparagus is a long-lived plant, and will continue to produce for well over twenty years in a suitable permanent location.

Harvested green and white asparagus

Bunch of Asparagus, *Édouard Manet, 1880*

Ornithogalum pyrenaicum

Prussian Asparagus

This wild flowering vegetable is a hardy European native. It is also known as Bath asparagus for its naturalized habitat in the woods and hedgerows around the city of Bath in western England. Other common names are Pyrenees star of Bethlehem and spiked star of Bethlehem. Wild Prussian asparagus is harvested for its young shoots and it is prepared and consumed in much the same way as cultivated asparagus. Tall, tightly budded spikes, which look a little like ears of green wheat, open to display pale, yellow-green, star-shaped flowers.

Tall flower spike

Cynara cardunculus

CARDOON

This spectacular thistlelike plant is a close relative of the artichoke and is more edible than it first appears. A popular European vegetable, the cardoon was introduced to the United States in the early 1800s, and it was a regular feature of the colonial kitchen garden. Today the cardoon is available in some farmer's markets and specialty grocery stores, but it is mostly grown for its large, showy flowers and considerable ornamental appeal.

Flower bud

Cooked cardoon stems

A POPULAR MEDITERRANEAN VEGETABLE

The cardoon is a drought-tolerant perennial native to southern Europe along the Mediterranean, where it was widely cultivated in ancient times. It is still valued as a wild food, and it is commercially produced in Spain, France, and Italy. Unopened cardoon buds can be eaten like small spiny artichokes, and the celerylike stalks are steamed, boiled, or braised. Cardoon stalks are a traditional Spanish Christmas vegetable, and cardoons feature in many North African cuisines. Cardoons cultivated for the table are blanched during growing to increase tenderness. The plants are bundled and wrapped with burlap about 18 inches high, and the soil is hilled around the plant. The stems have fine spines, so caution should be used when handling.

Celery is a popular vegetable with a wide range of culinary uses. The crunchy texture and aromatic nature of the vegetable in its raw state make it a favorite ingredient in salads, and its seeds are used as a seasoning.

A VARIED HISTORY

Thought to hail from the Mediterranean, celery is now grown throughout the world. A member of the Apiaceae family, it is an upright biennial plant with firm, ribbed leaves that grow in a rosette form. In ancient times it was used primarily as a medicinal and ceremonial plant—Egyptians placed celery garlands in burial chambers; Romans considered it to be an aphrodisiac. Around the fifteenth century, it began to be cultivated for culinary use.

Celery seeds and stalks

Culinary Uses

The distinctive flavor and many nutritional benefits of celery make it one of the best vegetables for juicing; with only six calories per stalk, it is a favorite among weight watchers. Celery is high in vitamin C and flavonoids, and its anti-inflammatory properties are especially beneficial to the digestive tract. Cooking celery significantly reduces its function as an antioxidant, so juicing is a great way to get the most out of this power vegetable. Celery juice can be consumed on its own or combined with other complementary vegetables and herbs, such as carrot, fennel, beets, cucumber, and mint.

Celery juice

Smallage

HEIRLOOM VARIETIES

Wild celery is known as "smallage." As its name suggests, it is smaller than cultivated celery, and it is more intensely aromatic. Its leaves can be used in salads and stews, but its stalks are stringy and have a harsh flavor, so the stalk is generally avoided. Among commercially produced celery in North America, the Pascal Giant variety reigns supreme due to its large size and compact form, but there are many other interesting varieties of this vegetable, including Golden Yellow, Golden Heart (also known as Kalamazoo), and the rare Pink Plume variety. One of the lesser-known heirloom varieties is red celery; it is easy to grow and considered by many to have a superior flavor.

WARNING! Celery belongs to a group of foods that can provoke severe allergic reactions or anaphylactic shock in some people. The allergens in celery do not lessen with cooking.

Allium schoenoprasum

CHIVES

The pretty, diminutive chive is the smallest of the flowering onion genus, and has a mild onion/garlic flavor. It produces clusters of tiny bulbs on underground rhizomes, and is easily propagated by dividing the rhizomes.

KITCHEN OR GARDEN PLANT

The chive is an attractive clump-forming plant with dark green tubular leaves, and it also produces clusters of pretty purple-pink flower heads. A popular perennial for the kitchen windowsill or herb garden, the chive is a cut-and-come-again plant. Removing flowers soon after blooming will encourage a second harvest later in the growing season. Dividing the plant every two years helps to maintain vigorous growth and prevent overcrowding. In the garden, the chive plant, like other species of the onion genus, is beneficial for its insect- and rodent-repelling properties. Its small habit makes it a useful rockery plant; grown en masse, it makes an attractive border plant.

Freshly snipped chives

Tiny chive bulbs

Culinary Uses

The leaves and flowers of the chive plant are used as a seasoning herb and as a fresh vegetable in salads, soups, and dips; chives are also used extensively as an edible garnish. The mildly pungent flavor and tender texture of chives make them a good accompaniment to eggs, as they do not overwhelm other delicate flavors. Chives combined with a little mustard makes a fragrant, lightly piquant sauce that is a good complement to chicken, pork, or fish. A simple cold version of this sauce can be made by combining yogurt, Dijon

Mustard chive sauce over fish

mustard, chives, sugar, and a little lemon juice. For a richer sauce, snipped chives are softened in a pan with butter, onion, and garlic. White wine, stock, and Dijon mustard are added, and the liquid is reduced by half. Cream is added to this and simmered until the desired consistency is reached.

Container garden with flowering chives

Allium ampeloprasum

ELEPHANT GARLIC

There are many popular vegetables belonging to the onion genus *Allium*. A number of these have similar or misleading names, which can create confusion. Elephant garlic is one example, since it is not a true garlic; it is one of three closely related cultivars of *Allium ampeloprasum* (the others are kurrat and leek), and it is botanically closer to the garden leek.

Giant clove of elephant garlic

A MILD HEAVYWEIGHT

The broad, straplike leaves of elephant garlic are similar in appearance to the garden leek. Unlike the leek, however, elephant garlic produces a large, segmented, compound bulb similar in appearance and taste to that of garlic. Despite its gigantic size—a single elephant garlic bulb can tip the scales at a pound in weight—the flavor of elephant garlic is much milder and a little sweeter than true garlic. It is prepared and cooked in much the same way, but care should be taken not to overcook it, as it is easily browned and will become bitter. Elephant garlic also has a shorter shelf life and a higher moisture and sugar content than garlic. The plant is easy to grow in the garden, and is also prized for its ornamental effect, producing striking inflorescences on single stalks.

Elephant garlic flower

Allium ampeloprasum var. *kurrat*

Kurrat

A close cousin of elephant garlic and leek, kurrat was first cultivated in the Middle East, and it has become widely naturalized. It is sometimes called Egyptian leek or broadleaf wild leek (not to be confused with the North American wild kurrat). It looks similar to a baby garden leek, and it is prepared and cooked as such. The whole plant can be eaten, including the bulb, leaves, and flowers. Kurrat leaves are more tender than leeks and can be eaten raw in salads or used as a garnish.

Dish with kurrat

Foeniculum vulgare var. *azoricum*

FLORENCE FENNEL

Florence fennel is a cultivar of aromatic wild fennel native to the Mediterranean. It belongs to the Apiaceae, or carrot family. Florence fennel is grown for its large aniseed-flavored "bulb" developed just above the ground, and for its edible stalks, foliage, and seeds. The bulb is actually a swollen leaf stem in thick, tightly packed layers.

FENNEL'S MANY USES

An attractive plant with a halo of wispy foliage, fennel produces large flower umbels up to 8 inches across, bearing clusters of tiny yellow flowers. All parts of the plant have an aniseed flavor to varying degrees; it is sweet in the bulb, more concentrated in the stalks, and mild in the leaves. The hairlike leaves of fennel are often mistaken for its cousin, dill, and can be used as a more mild-flavored substitute. Fennel leaves are used in salads and as a garnish, and are added to soups, stews, and egg dishes.

Yellow flower umbels

Fennel seeds

The stalks can be eaten like celery, although they are stringy. The strong, sweet flavor of fennel seeds gives Italian sausages their piquant flavor. Fennel seeds are also used in pickles, and in some countries chewed as an after-dinner snack. Florence fennel is more compact than its wild cousin, which can reach an impressive six feet in height. Cultivated fennel only grows to about two feet. It is a hardy perennial usually grown as an annual.

Culinary Uses

The crisp texture and refreshingly aromatic flavor of fennel makes it a perfect winter salad vegetable. Fennel and blood orange salad is a classic combination. Very thinly sliced or shaved fennel is layered with sliced blood oranges and mixed with a simple dressing made from the juice of the oranges and some olive oil. The salad may be finished with mint leaves or sliced hazelnuts.

Fennel and orange salad

Allium sativum

GARLIC

Garlic is a perennial herbaceous plant of the *Allium* genus, a huge category of plants containing hundreds of species, and it is closely related to onions, chives, and leeks. This aromatic vegetable was first cultivated in Central Asia. It has a long history as a culinary staple, as well as being used in traditional medicine.

HARDY GARDEN VEGETABLE

Garlic is an adaptable, easy-to-grow plant that produces segmented, edible bulbs. Its pretty pink and white flower heads are a pleasant addition to the garden, and they attract butterflies and bees. The leaves and flowers of the garlic plant are edible and the immature flower stalks, or scapes, are especially popular in some Southeast Asian countries, but the plant is mostly grown for its aromatic bulb. The hardy nature and natural antifungal defense system of the plant means that it is not susceptible to many diseases or pests

Garlic flower

in the garden. Two types of garlic are cultivated according to geographic location: hardneck garlic is grown in cooler climates, and softneck garlic is more suited to warmer climates. Softneck is the most common kind found in grocery stores.

String of garlic

Medicinal Uses

Before the development of modern pharmaceuticals, plants and other naturally occurring organic materials were used extensively as medicines. Garlic was used as a natural remedy for a wide range of ailments, as its antibacterial, antifungal, and antiseptic properties were well understood. Garlic contains an active sulfur compound called allicin, which is released when raw garlic is crushed, sliced, or chewed; this compound is also responsible for its pungent odor. The antimicrobial action of garlic has been borne out by modern science, and today garlic supplements are prescribed to help combat hypertension. Garlic also may help lower cholesterol, boost the immune system, and help prevent cell damage.

Harvesting garlic, from Tacuinum Sanitatis, *fifteenth century*

Roasted garlic

Crushed raw garlic cloves

GARLIC CHIVES

Allium tuberosum, or garlic chives, is a hardy, fast-growing, aggressively self-seeding plant of the onion family. It is native to China and Southeast Asia. In the United States it has naturalized in large parts of the Midwest, and it is considered an invasive weed. Other common names for this vegetable are Chinese chives or Chinese leeks. Its Asian names are *gau choy* (Chinese) and *nira* (Japanese).

PROCEED WITH CAUTION

Allium tuberosum produces clusters of umbels with beautiful, densely packed, fragrant flowers. They are a valuable addition to the garden for their ornamental beauty and for their ability to attract butterflies and pollinating bees. Their spreading habit makes them well suited to hard-to-fill crevices and rock gardens, although they can become invasive and hard to control if allowed to go to seed. As the common name suggests, its flavor is a blend of garlic and chives. Unlike true chives, however, the leaves of garlic chives are not tubular—they are flat and bladelike, and blue-green in color. Garlic chives are a popular vegetable throughout East Asia, where they are used in stir-fried dishes, soups, dumplings, pancakes, and pickled foods. All parts of the plant are edible, including the flowers and the black, peppery seeds that are produced.

Garlic chive flowers

Brassica oleracea var. *gongloydes*

KOHLRABI

Kohlrabi may look a lot like a turnip, but it is a cool-season cultivar of the cabbage family grown for its mild-flavored, swollen stem that develops just above ground level. It was first introduced in the United States at the beginning of the nineteenth century.

Raw kohlrabi grated in salad

ALIEN VEGETABLE

The rounded shape and cabbagelike form of this vegetable is summed up in its name, a derivation of the German compound word meaning "cabbage turnip." It has a crisp, juicy texture and a sweet flavor similar to broccoli stems. It is often grated or sliced and eaten raw—its crispy texture works especially well in coleslaws. Kohlrabi can also be cooked as a root vegetable, or added to stews and casseroles. In either case the thick, tough outer skin is peeled away as part of preparation. Kohlrabi leaves are also consumed as nutritious leafy greens. The leaves sprout straight from the swollen stem in a loose rosette pattern, giving the vegetable a somewhat bizarre appearance. Several colorful varieties are available, from white and pale green to vibrant purple.

Colorful varieties of kohlrabi in a market stall

Allium porrum

LEEK

The garden leek is a species of the onion genus *Allium*. Together with kurrat and elephant garlic, it is a cultivar of *Allium ampeloprasum*. Leek has a sweet, onionlike flavor without any of the pungency. While not fully hardy, this vegetable is more frost-tolerant than other onion cultivars.

MAXIMUM TENDERNESS
The leek does not develop a bulb; it is a compact bundle of leaves that transition from pure white at the base to dark bluish-green farther up the plant. The leaves are fleshy and straplike, arching out from the center in a symmetrical fan shape.

Trimmed leeks

Leek flower bud

The lower half to two-thirds of the plant is used in culinary dishes (the upper parts of the leaves are tough and fibrous, but may be used as a *bouquet garni*). The white part closest to the roots is the most tender, as it is blanched by the soil's protection from the sun. Hilling, or piling soil farther up the growing plant, will likewise produce a more tender vegetable. Small, tender leeks can be eaten raw, but they are more popular cooked as a green vegetable or added to casseroles and pies. A classic leek dish is vichyssoise, a cold, puréed soup made from leeks, onions, potatoes, and cream.

Braising sliced leeks

PRIDE OF WALES

The leek is a national emblem of Wales, deriving from a legendary battle between the seventh-century Welsh king Cadwaladr of Gwynedd and the Saxons. The battle took place in a leek field, and the king ordered his men to wear leeks on their helmets so that they may be distinguished from the enemy soldiers. Emblematic plants of the countries that make up the United Kingdom have been represented on the pound coin: the oak tree for England, the thistle for Scotland, flax for Northern Ireland, and the leek for Wales.

Pound coin with leek emblem

Cymbopogon citratus

LEMONGRASS

Synonymous with Thai food, lemongrass is an essential flavoring in Southeast Asian and Indian cuisines, and it is cultivated extensively throughout tropical Asia. Lemongrass is rich in oils that release their fragrance when crushed; another common name for this plant is oil grass.

AN ESSENTIAL OIL

Lemongrass belongs to the Poaceae family of grasses. It is fast-growing and forms an attractive, bushy mound of sharp, straplike, gracefully arching leaves, which have added ornamental appeal. In addition to its importance as a culinary plant, its leaves have been used for

Lemongrass growing in Thailand

centuries in the production of perfumes and traditional medicines. The active chemical compound responsible for the fresh citrus aroma of lemongrass is citral. Lemongrass extract is commercially available as an essential oil used in skin lotions, vaporizers, and as a massage or bath oil. It is also valued for its antimicrobial and antiseptic properties.

Culinary Uses

As important as lemongrass is to the flavor and character of many dishes, it is not actually consumed. The aromatic stalks and leaves are tough and do not break down when chewed, so they are set aside during the meal. A classic dish with lemongrass at its base is Thai coconut soup, *tom kha gai*. It can be made with shrimp or chicken combined with mushrooms, coconut milk, and lemongrass stalks. Seasonings for this dish vary, but will typically include lime juice, fish sauce, sugar, and chili paste, and it is often finished with basil leaves. Lemongrass is also a popular addition to teas, marinades, soups, and curries. It is nutritionally dense, and has a long shelf life in the refrigerator.

Chopped lemongrass stalks

Thai coconut soup, tom kha gai

Nelumbo nucifera

LOTUS ROOT

The gorgeous lotus may well steal the show as a fancy edible flower, but the leaves, seeds, and especially the lotus root are also used in a wide array of recipes in Asia.

Lotus is a warm-weather aquatic perennial. The huge flowers are short-lived, yet an individual lotus plant can survive for more than a thousand years, and spend years in a dormant state.

FLOATING HARVEST

Lotus leaves and flowers are produced on tall stems that hold the flower above the surface of the water. They are supported by an intensive root system growing in waterlogged soil. The lotus root—or more correctly, rhizome—is actually the submerged stem of the lotus plant. It has a thick, tubular form and a distinctive latticed interior. It is the most widely consumed part of the plant. As a fresh vegetable, lotus root has a crunchy texture and pleasant piquant flavor. It is sliced and added to salads and stir-fried dishes, prepared as chips, and consumed as a pickled vegetable. Lotus root can also be mashed and puréed, or ground into powder for use in cakes and confectionaries. The seeds are roasted and eaten like peanuts; dried lotus root is also popular as a tea.

Dish with sliced lotus root

Lotus seed head and seeds

Medicinal Uses

The lotus is a sacred plant in Asian cosmology (it is also commonly known as "sacred lotus"). It was one of the most revered medicinal plants in ancient China, where all parts of the plant had a medicinal application. Lotus was believed to rid the body of toxins and prevent overheating. The seeds were used to soothe the nerves and calm stomach upsets. Root powder was made into a paste and applied to ringworm and other skin conditions. Lotus root is known to have styptic and astringent actions, and it has natural antiseptic properties. It is nutritionally dense, containing a potent mix of vitamins and minerals, including calcium, iron, copper, zinc, magnesium, and manganese, which are beneficial to the production of red blood cells. It has an antioxidant action, and it provides a good source of fiber.

Lotus root

LOTUS GALLERY

Commonly referred to as lotus "root," this striking vegetable is actually the submerged rhizome of the plant. The flowers, leaves, and seeds are also edible.

1

2

3

4

1: Lotus rhizomes; 2: Sliced lotus root; 3: Seed head; 4: Lotus flower; 5: Dried lotus root; 6: Segmented rhizomes; 7: Lotus leaves

Opuntia ficus-indica

NOPAL

Spiny nopal is a species of edible cactus native to Mexico, and it is eaten both as a fruit and as a vegetable. Nopal is commonly known as prickly pear, cactus pear, and barbary fig. The word for the paddle-shaped pads, *nopales*, is derived from the Aztec word *nohpalli*. The nopal cactus is widely cultivated in arid and semiarid countries around the world.

Nopales ready for sale in Morocco

Mexican market trader

FLESHY VEGETABLE

The spiny leaf pads, or nopales, are a popular vegetable in Mexico, where they grow in abundance. It is also becoming more available in the southwestern United States. The nopal cactus thrives in hot desert

Nopales with fruit

conditions where it cross-pollinates and easily propagates. Nopales have a thick, fleshy texture and a slightly tart flavor reminiscent of asparagus or green beans. They are harvested while young, before the spines have hardened, and are eaten raw in salads or cooked in stews. Small nopales are called *nopalitos*. Commercially produced nopales may be purchased prepeeled or canned. They are typically sliced and cooked as a green vegetable, but they are also used in jams, candies, and smoothies. Like okra, nopales have a mucilaginous action and are a natural thickener in soups and stews.

Culinary Uses

Nopales rellenos, or stuffed nopales, is a popular Mexican dish. It is a simple recipe—most of the work involved is in preparing the nopales. The spines must be carefully removed using a knife or potato peeler (it is advisable to wear gloves while doing this). The pads are boiled until just tender, and then slices of Oaxacan cheese and onion are sandwiched between two nopales and secured with cocktail sticks. The whole thing is then dipped in a batter of whisked eggs, and then fried until golden brown. Nopales rellenos may be served served with salsa.

Removing nopal pad spines

Allium cepa

ONION

The best-known and most widely grown species of the *Allium* genus is the common onion, a beloved vegetable adapted to innumerable cuisines worldwide. Cultivated at least since written records began, onions have come a long way from their ancestral origins. Today they are available in a wide variety of shapes, sizes, flavors, and colors.

ONIONS FOR EVERYTHING

Historically, the onion has been put to a great variety of uses, in medicine, cuisine, and far beyond. To the ancient Egyptians the concentric layers of the onion symbolized eternal life. They placed

Red onions

onions in the burial chambers of pharaohs and sometimes directly onto the entombed bodies. Onionskins were widely used throughout Europe to dye textiles and wool yarns. In medicinal folklore the onion was prescribed as treatment for ailments as far-ranging as snakebites and balding. In

Egyptian tomb painting of onion harvesting

medieval England it was believed to draw out poisons and ward off the plague. Modern research has shown the onion to have antiseptic and antibacterial properties.

Allium ampeloprasum var. *sectivum*

Pearl Onion

The diminutive pearl onion is a species of *Allium* with a misleading name. It is not a true onion, but is closely related to the leek. Pearl onions are available in attractive white, gold, and red varieties. They are especially popular in northern Europe as a pickled vegetable; in the United States they are often purchased frozen. Raw pearl onions can be difficult and time-consuming to peel; blanching them first helps the skins to slip off more easily.

Pickled pearl onions

ALLIUM GALLERY

The *Allium* genus contains many species of onion, and other pungent bulb vegetables, such as leeks, chives, and garlic. Alliums produce flowers on scapes that emerge directly from the bulb.

1

2

3

1: Shallots; 2: Common onions; 3: Garlic bulbs; 4: Cipollini onions; 5: French red onions; 6: Pearl onions; 7: Spring onions; 8: Globe allium flower

Allium tricoccum

RAMPS

Ramps is an Appalachian "forager's" name for *Allium tricoccum*, which is also called wild leek, wood leek, wild garlic, ramp, and spring onion. Ramps are not cultivated, they are harvested from the wild. Their increasing popularity means that they are now at risk of overharvesting. The Latin subspecies name, *tricoccum*, refers to the way the plant produces seeds in triplet form.

APPALACHIAN SPRING

Ramps are native to the northeastern United States and can be found growing freely in moist, loamy soil near streams and in forests. They are recognizable by their broad, glossy leaves and reddish stalks. The leaves die back in June before the plant produces flowers and seeds. Ramps have a mild

Ramps in flower

Ramps in seed

onion flavor and a garlic scent; the bulbs are slender and white. Historically, ramps were prized as the first nutritious greens to appear after the long winter's dearth of fresh fruits and vegetables. Considered a tonic for many cold-weather ailments, the vitamins and minerals in ramps helped boost the general health of those who went without the benefit of fresh produce for long periods. They were widely harvested by Native Americans, and today festivals in Appalachia—and many parts of the eastern and southeastern United States—still celebrate the appearance of ramps as signifying the arrival of spring. Ramps festivals feature traditional ramps dishes and cook-offs against a backdrop of regional music and dance.

deep-
fried
batter-
dipped ramps

Traditional festival food

Allium cepa var. *aggregatum*

SHALLOT

The shallot is a species of small onion that produces clusters of irregular shaped offsets, or cloves, from a single "parent" bulb. The Latin name *aggregatum,* plus other common names for this plant—ever-ready onion and multiplier onion—indicate its cumulative habit. A single bulb planted just below the ground will produce six to eight additional bulbs of equal size.

A GOURMET ONION

The shallot is often referred to as *échalote,* a derivation of its French name. The shallot has a milder, more refined flavor than the onion, but it is equally hardy in the garden. Its slender, pointed bulbs come in a variety of colors, from red- or copper-skinned to pink, white, and gray-skinned cultivars.

Distinctive pink-tinged flesh

The flesh often has a distinctive pink tinge. Shallots are available in three sizes: jumbo, medium, and small; smaller shallots are considered to have superior flavor. The subtle, aromatic flavor of shallots makes them well suited for use as a raw vegetable. The long, hollow leaves are also edible (as are the flowers) and can be used in salads, soups, and stews.

Bunch of French red shallots

Allium fistulosum

WELSH ONION

The Welsh onion is a perennial herb native to Asia and not, as one might assume, to Wales. Its name is misleading; "Welsh," in this case, is believed to derive either from the Old English word *welisc*, or the Old German word *welsche* which simply means "foreign."

Welsh onions were introduced into Europe in the seventeenth century. They are still popular in Europe today, and they are also widely used in Asian cuisines. Welsh onion is best known as bunching onion in Japan, and scallion or green onion in the United States.

YEAR-ROUND HARVEST

The Welsh onion has attractive, hollow, tubelike leaves. Unlike the garden onion, it does not produce a rounded bulb; instead, it develops a white, elongated thickening at the base of the stem, and it multiplies by division. Many cultivars of Welsh onion have been developed for their relative hardiness, heat tolerance, flavor, and color. It is a fast-growing, easy-to-manage plant, and as a cold-tolerant evergreen perennial, it is one of the few vegetables that can be harvested year-round. Welsh onion has a milder flavor than the garden onion and is used raw in salads, or it is lightly cooked in stir- or flash-fried dishes. It is also used as an herb to flavor soups and stews.

Emerging Welsh onion flower

Agaricus bisporus

MUSHROOM

You may be wondering why mushrooms are included in a book on vegetables, since mushrooms are a fungus and not a vegetable, and do not even belong to the plant kingdom. They are, however, commonly eaten as a vegetable.

THE COMMON MUSHROOM

Agaricus bisporus, or the common mushroom, belongs to a large family of fungi known as Agaricaceae, which is native to Europe and North America. It is the most widely cultivated mushroom, and it accounts for 90 percent of commercial mushroom production in the United States. The common mushroom is *Agaricus bisporus*, in its immature state, and is available in white or brown closed-cap form, marketed as white, brown, or button mushrooms.

Harvested mushrooms, packaged for sale

Dark-gilled portobello mushrooms

Mature *Agaricus bisporus* is known as a portobello mushroom. It is simply the common mushroom allowed to grow beyond the button stage. It has a stronger flavor and an open cap that reveals dark gills.

A COMPOST FOOD

Unlike plants, mushrooms are heterotrophic and cannot make their own nutrients. Instead they must take their nutrients from composted materials with high nitrogen content, typically horse manure and straw. Fungi are natural decomposers that break down other organic materials. Some species of edible fungi have evolved different strategies for obtaining nutrients. Many can be found growing as parasites on host trees or tree stumps, or on manure and naturally composting materials. Some fungi are carnivorous, such as the oyster mushroom *(Pleurotus ostreatus)* and caterpillar fungus *(Ophiocordyceps sinensis)*, which derive their nutrients from the insects they kill.

WARNING! "All mushrooms are edible, but some only once," is a Croatian proverb that should not be taken lightly. While the common mushroom is easily found growing wild in grasslands and meadows, great care must be taken not to confuse it with the highly poisonous destroying angel (Amanita virosa), whose white, rounded form can look like a button mushroom. The destroying angel is one of the most dangerous and deadly poisonous fungi. It can be identified by its snow-white gills.

Poisonous destroying angel

MUSHROOM GALLERY

Mushrooms are a fungi that is typically consumed as a vegetable. They are both foraged in the wild and commercially produced, and come in a dazzling variety of shapes, colors, and forms. Some species are poisonous.

1: Oyster mushrooms; 2: Enokitake;
3: Shiitake mushrooms; 4: Button mushrooms;
5: Portobello mushrooms; 6: Lion's Mane
mushroom; 7: Porcini mushroom

CHAPTER 5

ROOT & TUBEROUS VEGETABLES

Beta vulgaris ssp. vulgaris

BEETROOT

Modern beetroot, also called garden beet or simply beet, was developed from wild sea beet (*Beta maritima*), which grows freely along the coastlines and marshlands of Europe, North Africa, and Asia. Beetroot is a biennial vegetable sown in the spring and harvested before the intense heat of summer.

A SWEET VEGETABLE

The high sugar content and mild flavor of beetroot make it especially palatable to children and adaptable to a wide variety of dishes. The root can be consumed thinly sliced or grated and added to salads and sandwiches, or it can be boiled or roasted and eaten as a fresh vegetable. Beetroot is extremely popular as a relish or chutney, pickled in vinegar with various spices, or fermented as wine. The leaves of the plant are edible and also highly palatable, similar in texture and taste to Swiss chard or spinach, and they can be cooked in much the same way.

There are a number of different color varieties of beetroot, from the classic deep red, to orange, pink, white, and striped.

Beetroot varieties

Culinary Uses

A classic eastern European traditional dish is *borscht*, a hearty beetroot soup of dazzling red hue. There are vegetarian and nonvegetarian versions—the latter usually includes beef or bacon—and innumerable regional variations. Simply put, cooked beets and potatoes are added to a large pan with sautéed onions and cabbage, chicken stock, a little lemon juice, and the seasonings bay leaf, fresh dill, salt, and pepper. The soup is cooked further until the flavors merge, and it is served with a dollop of sour cream. Beetroot releases a great deal of pigmented juice when cut, which can be a nuisance, as it stains skin, clothes, and other porous surfaces. Leaving the skin of the beetroot intact during cooking will help minimize this.

Borscht

Beetroot juice

Arctium lappa

BURDOCK

This thistlelike plant is native to Europe and Asia, and has naturalized in parts of North America. It grows wild along roadsides, riverbanks, and in fields, and is seldom cultivated. The bristly heads are avoided as a food by most animals, but the stems and long, skinny taproots are a palatable and nutritious vegetable. Burdock root is popular in Japan, where it is known as *gobo*. The young stalks of this plant can be served as a fresh vegetable and have a flavor similar to asparagus or artichoke heart.

Burdock flower

THE ORIGINAL VELCRO

The name *burdock* is a compound of the French word *bourre*, in reference to its bristly burrs, and the Middle English word *dokke*, for its large, coarse leaves that are similar to the weedy dock leaf. The burrs have hooked tips and can attach themselves to the wool or fur of passing animals (or the clothes of passing humans) as an effective manner of dispersing seeds. The natural adhesive ability of this plant inspired

Spiny burs known as beggars' buttons

the inventor of Velcro, George de Mestral, after he observed this action while walking with his dog. The burdock plant produces copious attractive purple flowers and the leaves can grow to great size. The roots are harvested when they are about twelve inches long and about one inch in diameter.

Dried burdock root

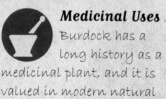 ### Medicinal Uses

Burdock has a long history as a medicinal plant, and it is valued in modern natural medicines for its antibacterial, antifungal, and anti-inflammatory properties. The leaves, seeds, and roots are used to treat a number of ailments. It is most commonly used as a blood purifier, a diuretic, and to improve blood circulation. It is also used to treat skin complaints such as eczema and psoriasis, and to promote healthy liver function. Burdock extract is available as a homeopathic medicine or herbal supplement, and dried burdock root is produced as a tea.

Burdock flowers pressed into oil

Daucus carota ssp. sativus

CARROT

The carrot has been cultivated for millennia. The earliest forms had dark purple roots; the vibrant orange-hued carrot of today was not developed until the seventeenth century. The carrot is a staple vegetable cultivated across much of the globe.

A CLASSIC VEGETABLE

Carrot seems to be synonymous with the color orange, but there are also purple, white, yellow, and red varieties. The taproots can grow up to twenty inches in length, but they are generally harvested before growing too large, as the flesh can become fibrous. Short-rooted dwarf varieties are also available. The carrot is a hardy biennial; left in the ground to mature, it will flower in its second year. As a cultivated food crop,

Freshly harvested carrots

it is harvested in the first year before it has a chance to flower. Wild carrot produces umbels of lacy white flowers on tall stems, known as Queen Anne's lace. Carrots feature heavily in children's literature, from classics like Beatrix Potter's *The Tale of Peter Rabbit*, published in 1901, to Ruth Krauss's *The Carrot Seed*, first published in 1945.

Queen Anne's lace

Culinary Uses

Carrots can be boiled, mashed, roasted, caramelized, and eaten raw in salads and sandwiches. The sweet, mild flavor and cheerful color make it a popular vegetable among children, especially when it appears in the form of a cake. Carrot cake is made with traditional cake mix proportions of butter, flour, and eggs, but the addition of grated carrot means that less sugar is needed to sweeten the mix. Carrot also adds a pleasant moistness to the cake, which is traditionally served with cream cheese frosting.

Carrot cake

CARROT GALLERY

The carrot has come a long way from its humble wild ancestor, and is available today in a variety of forms and a rainbow of colors. Worldwide, carrots rank second only in popularity to the potato.

1: Purple carrots; 2: Variety of heirloom carrots;
3: Yellow cultivars; 4: Sliced heirloom purple carrot;
5: Heirloom round and purple carrots; 6: Common
garden carrot

Manihot esculenta

CASSAVA

Cassava is a drought-tolerant perennial of the Euphorbiaceae, or spurge family, grown for its long, starchy tubers. It is an important food crop throughout Africa and the tropics and subtropics, with Nigeria leading in commercial production.

LIFE-GIVING CASSAVA

Cassava was a staple food among pre-Columbian peoples, and it is a vital food in developing countries today. In its cultural and culinary significance it may be compared to bread; indeed, one West African name for this vegetable translates as "there is life." Other common names include yuca, tapioca, mandioca, and manihot. Cassava is thought to have originated in the forests of South America. The attractive leaves are large and palmate.

Smooth white flesh of cassava root

Cassava roots

Culinary Uses

Cassava tubers are dense and heavy, weighing a pound or more each. The rich, brown skins are tough, and the firm flesh is bright white. Cassavas have a fibrous core, which is not eaten. Despite this, cassavas bruise easily, so they may be found in grocery stores in a protective wax coating. Cassava is a highly versatile vegetable that takes many culinary forms. It can be cooked in all of the ways root vegetables are typically prepared. It can also be made into flour, processed to make tapioca pearls, fried as chips, or fermented as beer. A popular West African dish is *fufu*, a savory preparation with a puddinglike consistency, made by pounding boiled cassava with a little water. Cassava also has industrial applications in the manufacture of plywood, glue, textiles, and paper.

African fufu

WARNING!
Cassava tubers contain small amounts of toxic cyanogenic glycosides. If eaten raw or extensively over a long period, consumption can lead to cyanide poisoning. The toxins are concentrated in the skin and outer flesh, so the tubers are rendered safe by peeling and then boiling thoroughly.

Apium graveolens var. *rapaceum*

CELERIAC

Celeriac is also known as celery root or knob celery. It is a member of the Apiaceae, or carrot family, and it is hardier and more frost- and disease-resistant than its close relative, celery. Celeriac is cultivated for its swollen stem base (hypocotyl), which is harvested when it reaches three to four inches in size.

AN UNDERAPPRECIATED VEGETABLE

Celeriac is a popular vegetable among Europeans, and widely grown in temperate parts of Europe, Asia, and Africa; however, it is less common in the United States, possibly due to its unattractive appearance. The rough, knobby exterior and tangle of wispy roots are peeled before eating. The flavor of celeriac is described as a blend of celery, turnip, and parsley. It is an adaptable vegetable with white flesh and a smooth flavor. Its woody exterior means it has a long shelf life, and it will keep for months if stored in cool conditions. Celeriac is eaten raw in salads, or cooked much as other winter root vegetables. It can be boiled, roasted, fried, mashed, or puréed and added to soups and stews. The leaves and seeds are edible, and the leaf stalks may be eaten like celery, but the flavor is intense, so the stalks are often reserved for seasoning. The raw flesh of celeriac has a crisp texture and quickly discolors when exposed to the air.

Celeriac root

Celeriac cream soup

Stachys affinis

CHINESE ARTICHOKE

Chinese artichoke is an herbaceous plant grown for its small, tasty, edible rhizomes. It is a member of the wide-ranging Lamiaceae, or mint family, and its wrinkled foliage bears a strong resemblance to spearmint.

WORTH THE EFFORT

Stachys affinis has numerous common names, including crosne, chorogi, and knotroot—the latter being perhaps the most appropriate, since the convoluted form of this root vegetable makes cleaning it a somewhat onerous task for the cook. Chinese artichoke may be the most flattering name for this peculiar vegetable as it has all the appearance of large, white grubs. It is mostly found in specialty grocery stores in the United States, but like its cousin mint, it is easy to grow and is less invasive in the garden. Chinese artichoke is a popular vegetable in France and may be found on menus in the United States under its French name, *crosnes* (pronounced "crone"). The roots have a nutty flavor and crunchy texture, similar to water chestnuts. In China and Japan it is often served pickled, and is used in stir-fried dishes, soups, and stews. Chinese artichoke may be eaten raw in salads or simply braised as a fresh vegetable.

Cleaned Chinese artichokes

Pickled Chinese artichokes

Raphanus sativus var. *longipinnatus*

DAIKON

Daikon, also known as Japanese radish, is a handsome vegetable easily identified on grocery store shelves for its elongated, smooth white tubers. The plant originated in Southeast Asia, and is widely grown throughout Asia. It is a cruciferous vegetable of the Brassicaceae, or cabbage family.

MANY USES OF DAIKON

Daikon root has dense flesh with a high water content. Individual radishes weigh anywhere from one to two pounds each. Daikon radishes can grow up to twenty inches in length, but they are generally harvested when the tubers reach twelve inches. Daikon has a mildly pungent flavor and a juicy texture that works well with pickling. It is a high-fiber vegetable that is rich in vitamin C. It can be cooked in stir-fries and stews, but it is also eaten raw in a wide variety of preparations. It is shaved and added to salads and condiments, and is widely used as a garnish. It is an excellent addition to coleslaw, and can be roasted as a root vegetable. Grated daikon is also steeped as a tea. Daikon leaves are edible and have a similarly pungent flavor; they can be eaten like the leafy greens spinach, chard, and kale. Many varieties of daikon are sold throughout Asia, including globular turnip-shaped forms and the beautiful green-skinned heirloom cultivar, watermelon radish, which has deep pink flesh. Other types have black, pink, or purple skin.

Harvested daikon

Watermelon radish

Amorphophallus paeoniifolius

ELEPHANT FOOT YAM

No prizes for guessing how this vegetable got its name—indeed, it bears an uncanny resemblance to an elephant's foot. Other common names are whitespot giant arum and stink lily—the plant gives off a putrid smell of rotting meat, which attracts pollinating flies.

HEAVYWEIGHT YAM

Elephant foot yam is a heat-loving, tropical perennial native to India and Sri Lanka. It is grown for its large, edible corms, commonly referred to as tubers. The corms can weigh in at about two to six pounds, but can be as heavy as thirty pounds. Elephant foot yam is a starchy vegetable with pale flesh that is similar in color, flavor, and texture to sweet potato. It is usually roasted or boiled, and is always eaten cooked. It is used in India and Bangladesh in curries, pickles, and chutneys. Elephant foot yam is slow to mature and does not produce a flower until the third or fourth year.

Edible corm

WARNING! Eaten raw, this plant can cause a severe irritation in the mouth and throat; boiling thoroughly neutralizes the harmful properties. Handling the plant with bare hands may also cause skin irritation.

Halved elephant foot yam

Ensete ventricosum

ENSETE

This impressive, large-leafed perennial is also known as Ethiopian or Abyssinian banana. It is a drought-tolerant plant native to tropical East Africa, and is widely cultivated in Ethiopia, where it has been a staple food for 5,000 years.

WHOLE HARVEST PLANT

Unlike its cousin the "true" banana, which is cultivated for its yellow fruits, ensete is grown exclusively as a vegetable, and it is an essential source of carbohydrates and calories for large populations living in drought-prone areas. Its thick, tightly clustered pseudostems are pounded into flour, or fermented as kocho, a starchy paste that forms the basis for a number of foods. Its underground, starchy rhizomes are cooked much like a potato. The tender tissue at the plant's core is highly palatable, and is similar to hearts of palm. The fruit is insignificant and flavorless. Ensete is not grown as a food crop outside of Africa; however, dwarf cultivars of this plant are sold for ornamental use, and their huge, ribbed leaves provide architectural interest in the garden.

Pulped ensete in fermenting pit

Ensete flower

Zingiber officinale

GINGER

Ginger is a tropical perennial that originated in Asia, where it has long played a central role as a culinary vegetable and a traditional medicine. It is widely cultivated for its sweetly pungent, aromatic rhizome, or swollen underground stem.

Ginger crop plantation

Sliced ginger root

EAST AND WEST

This aromatic, spicy vegetable is used extensively throughout Asia, where it lends its unique flavor and pleasant aroma to a wide variety of dishes. The culinary uses of ginger are too many to enumerate; it has worldwide popularity in both savory and sweet dishes. Ginger may be crystalized as candy; used to flavor cakes, cookies, and curries; and it gives Caribbean ginger beer its distinctive kick. It is also a familiar sight in the East and the West as an essential accompaniment to sushi, where it is served pickled and thinly sliced. The leaves of the ginger plant are stiff and reedlike, and the pale yellow flowers are cone shaped. Cultivated ginger is rarely allowed to flower.

Flower of the ginger plant

Pickled sushi ginger

Medicinal Uses

The boon of pregnant women, ginger is a natural way to stave off nausea and help suppress vomiting. It also helps to alleviate nausea caused by chemotherapy, surgery, and motion sickness. Ginger has an ancient history as a digestive medicine in Asia, and its anti-inflammatory properties have also helped those suffering from muscle and joint pain caused by arthritis. The active chemicals in ginger are gingerol, shogaol, and zingerone (which are also responsible for its pungency). Studies suggest that this plant may be useful in treating heart disease and may have a role in the search for effective cancer treatments. Ginger as a therapeutic medicine can be taken in a number of ways: it may be eaten as a raw food, taken as an extract, or dried and processed as a pill, a powder, or an infusion.

Armoracia rusticana

HORSERADISH

Horseradish is a hardy perennial native to Europe and Asia. It is grown mainly for its spicy roots, but the young leaves are also edible and make an interesting addition to salads. Horseradish is a member of the Brassicaceae family, which contains the similarly pungent plants mustard and wasabi.

CHEMICAL REACTION

The source of horseradish's pungency is the volatile oil allyl isothiocyanate, which is produced when the roots or leaves are cut into; this chemical reaction is the plant's natural defense mechanism against grazing animals. Horseradish is easy to grow in the garden, but it can be highly invasive and difficult to eradicate once established. For this reason, many people prefer to grow it only in pots. The plant produces fragrant, small white flowers. The roots are ready for harvesting in the fall. Once harvested, horseradish roots can be stored in cool, dry conditions for months.

Harvested horseradish roots

Culinary Uses

Horseradish is a popular condiment throughout Europe and the United States. In the UK, horseradish sauce is a traditional accompaniment to roast beef; in the United States it is a favorite with prime rib. In eastern European countries traditional relishes often pair the pungency of horseradish with the sweetness of red beets and regional spices. To make homemade horseradish sauce, simply combine grated fresh horseradish with sour cream or mayonnaise, Dijon mustard, and a little white wine vinegar, and blend in a food processor until it reaches the desired consistency. Season the blended mixture with salt and pepper. Freshly grated horseradish will turn brown when exposed to the air, but adding vinegar to the mixture will prevent this.

Grated horseradish

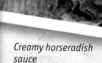

Creamy horseradish sauce

WARNING!
Caution should be taken when grating horseradish, as it can irritate the eyes and lining of the nose. Grating should be done in a well-ventilated space. Ingesting large amounts of this plant can be poisonous.

Red horseradish sauce

Tropaeolum tuberosum

MASHUA

Mashua is a tall, flowering perennial native to Ecuador, Colombia, Bolivia, and Peru, long cultivated in the Andes for its edible tubers. It is a nutritious, high-yield, vigorous climbing plant, well adapted to high altitudes, and it can thrive even in poor soils. It is also pest- and disease-resistant, and is often grown as a companion plant to potato to help protect the crop from damage by pests and pathogens.

MIXED REPUTATION

The colorful, cone-shaped tubers of the mashua plant are pungent and peppery tasting. They are served raw, boiled, or roasted, which reduces their pungency. Mashua is a relative of the *nasturtium* species and has a similar peppery taste found in edible nasturtium leaves. Mashua's flowers are equally pretty; it is often grown as an ornamental plant prized for attracting hummingbirds

Trumpet form of mashua flowers

to the garden. Mashua has a reputation as an antiaphrodisiac dating back to Inca civilizations, when it was fed to Inca armies with the aim of suppressing sexual desire. In some rural parts of the Andes, mashua is avoided by men who believe it causes impotence.

Halved mashua root

Petroselinum crispum var. *tuberosum*

PARSLEY ROOT

Similar in appearance to baby parsnips, the edible taproots of *Petroselinum crispum* var. *tuberosum* are long and skinny, and have a nutty, celery-like flavor. Parsley root is a member of the same botanical family as the carrot (Apiaceaea). It is native to the Mediterranean, and is widely naturalized across Europe.

OLD WORLD VEGETABLE

This plant first became popular as a root vegetable in Germany in the sixteenth century—hence one of its common names, Hamburg parsley—and it continues to be a favorite winter vegetable in Germany, Austria, Holland, Poland, and Russia. It is not easily found in the United States, but is easy to grow from seed in the garden. Parsley root is prepared and cooked in much the same way as parsnip, but it is considered sweeter and milder. Its leaves are also edible, with an intense parsley flavor. They are typically used in winter salads and as a garnish, or to season soups and stews.

Freshly grated parsley root

Pastinaca sativa

PARSNIP

Parsnip is the sweet, nutty taproot of *Pastinaca sativa*, a member of the Apiaceae, or carrot family. It is an herbaceous perennial native to Eurasia, widely consumed across northern Europe.

AN EARLY SWEETENER

Parsnip is a beloved winter vegetable in the UK, and is an integral part of the traditional Sunday roast (it is not, however, a popular table vegetable in Italy, where parsnips are instead fed to pigs bred for Parma ham). The high sugar content in parsnip is comparable to grapes and bananas. Before the introduction of cane sugar in Europe, it was used to sweeten jams and cakes. Parsnips can be eaten raw, but are typically cooked, which increases their sweetness. Thinly sliced parsnips can also be fried as chips. Parsnip is easy to grow from seed in the garden, where some plants may be left in the ground to flower and produce seeds for a future crop. The flower umbels have small, yellow-green petals. Like many winter root vegetables, parsnips are sweetest when harvested after the first frost. Second-growth roots are woody and not good for eating. Parsnips may be harvested and stored in a cool place, or parboiled and frozen.

Peeled parsnips

Culinary Uses

The mild, nutty flavor of parsnip lends itself to creamy soups, which are satisfying both in their simplicity and ease of preparation. Braised parsnips, potatoes, and shallots are simmered in water until tender, then blended with heavy cream to a smooth consistency. All that remains is to season the soup with salt and pepper, and finish it with sliced almonds.

Roasted parsnips

WARNING!
The leaves and shoots of the parsnip plant contain the toxic chemical compound furanocoumarin, which is a natural defense mechanism of the plant. Contact with the skin can cause a chemical burn resulting in redness and blistering. The chemical is not present in the roots.

Parsnip soup

Conopodium majus

PIGNUT

Pignut is a lesser-known root vegetable of the Apiaceae, or carrot family, and it grows wild in Europe and parts of North Africa. It is prized as a forage food and may be harvested from forestlands, hedgerows, and undisturbed grasslands. The "nut" of the pignut is a small rhizomatous tuber, or corm, that looks like a chestnut, and it has a pleasant, nutty taste. The plant gets its name from its popularity among pigs. It is also called hognut, earthnut, and Saint Anthony's nut. The pignut plant has feathery leaves, and it bears umbels of tiny, white flowers. Care must be taken in identifying this wild food, as it often grows among bluebells, whose bulbs are poisonous.

Pignut plant

Solanum tuberosum

POTATO

The wild potato is native to South America, and was first domesticated by Inca people in Peru between 8,000 and 5,000 BC. The potato plant is a member of the Solanaceae, or nightshade family.

Potato flowers

HISTORIC VEGETABLE

The potato was introduced from South America to Europe in the sixteenth century, and it first entered the United States in 1621. By the early eighteenth century, it was firmly established as a food crop. In Europe, because of its adaptability, high yield, and nutritional content, the potato replaced many traditional crops and became a staple of the poor. In nineteenth-century Ireland, potato cultivation was dominated by a single variety. The almost complete dependency on the potato among the working class in Ireland meant widespread famine and the deaths of approximately one million people when a fungal blight decimated the crops. Today the potato is the world's most important root crop.

Botanical illustration of potato plant, artist unknown, 1907

Culinary Uses

In addition to the ubiquitous French fry, there are innumerable diverse uses for the potato, and many of the best are of French origin: Duchess potatoes (pommes de terre duchesse) and gratin Dauphinoise to name but two.

Potatoes Anna

Another historical French dish is pommes Anna, which dates back to Napoleonic Paris. It is made from thin-sliced potatoes dried on paper towels, and then layered in a heavy pan with butter, salt, and pepper. The potatoes are cooked on the stovetop until golden brown, then the pan is transferred to the oven where the potatoes will caramelize. The whole thing is tipped upside down onto a plate and served in slices.

WARNING!
All green parts of the potato plant, including green unripe tubers, contain the toxic compound alkaloid solanine, which is present in species of the nightshade family. Ingesting green parts of the plant will result in poisoning.

POTATO GALLERY

Americans eat more potatoes than any other vegetable. More than one hundred varieties are available nationwide, while thousands are grown worldwide.

1: Apache potatoes; 2: Red, white, and purple varieties; 3: Young white potatoes; 4: Red cultivars; 5: Pink Fir Apple potatoes; 6: Mixed cultivars; 7: Purple and white potatoes

Psoralea esculenta

PRAIRIE TURNIP

This little plant grows wild on the prairies and in the woodlands of North America. Called *timpsula* by Native American Sioux, the prairie turnip was an essential food crop for Native Americans living on the Great Plains. It is also known as Indian breadroot. Prairie turnip is a perennial plant of the Fabaceae, or pea and bean family.

FINDERS KEEPERS!

Prairie turnip produces abundant tubers underground. The spindle-shaped tubers are roughly the size of a hen's egg. They are a palatable and nutritious vegetable, high in protein and rich in vitamin C. They may be cooked in the same ways as potatoes, but their flavor is described as being like a slightly sweet turnip. Easily identified on the prairie because of their pretty purple flowers, they were harvested in great numbers by Native American women, and were consumed fresh, or stored for later use and traded for other foods. The women would make a game of the search, telling their children that timpsula point at each other. The children would follow the direction of the leaves and help in the search for more plants. Dried prairie roots would be pounded into flour; today prairie turnip flour is often used to make frybread, a traditional Native American food.

Spindle-shaped tuber

Native American frybread

Raphanus sativus

RADISH

The wild ancestry of the radish is unknown, but historians believe it originated in Southeast Asia where wild forms of the plant exist, and it was domesticated in Europe in pre-Roman times. It is a cool-season biennial plant of the Brassicacea, or cabbage family.

NIGHT OF THE RADISHES

There is a long tradition of vegetable carving in Asian cuisine, and the radish is a particular favorite, carved into simple or wildly elaborate food decorations. In Mexico radishes are carved with religious themes and are displayed in the annual Christmas market on December 23, a short-lived event known as Night of the Radishes. Radishes are broadly divided into

Carved green radish

winter and spring or summer varieties. The common, globular red type is sometimes referred to as European radish; other varieties may be elongated or pear-shaped, and may have black, white, orange, pink, or green skins. The entire radish plant is edible, including the seeds. The leaves can be braised as leafy greens, but most often it is grown for its swollen taproot. The radish plant is generally grown from seed as an annual, but if it is left in the ground to mature, it will flower and provide seeds for the next crop. The cruciform flowers are pale pink or purple. It grows quickly; some varieties produce an edible crop as early as three weeks after germination.

Sliced radishes and radish flowers

Brassica napus var. *napobrassica*

RUTABAGA

Rutabaga is a member of the large Brassicaceae, or cabbage family, and is also called swede or yellow turnip. Its blue-green leaves are very similar to those of cabbage. Rutabaga is not a naturally occurring plant; it is a hybrid of the turnip and wild cabbage.

IN HONOR OF THE POET

Rutabaga is a hardy cool-season vegetable. It is easy to grow and requires little maintenance in the garden. It is grown primarily for its large, fleshy taproot, or hypocotyl; the leaves of the plant are edible, but only very young leaves are palatable. The bulbous taproots are harvested after the first frost (this improves their sweetness), when they have grown three to five inches in diameter. Left in the ground, they become woody and bland as they mature, so it is better to harvest them early and store them in a cool, dark place for later use. Rutabaga has a dull, orange-purple exterior and buttery yellow flesh with a mild, sweet flavor. Like most winter root vegetables, it can be boiled, roasted, fried, mashed, or puréed, and used in a wide range of soups, casseroles, and stews. Rutabaga can also be consumed raw, in which case it is best grated or julienned. In Scotland, mashed rutabaga, or neeps, is the traditional accompaniment to haggis, which is eaten on Burns' Night in honor of Scotland's national poet, Robert Burns.

Halved rutabaga

Traditional Scottish neeps with haggis

Tragopogon porrifolius

SALSIFY

Today salsify is largely a forage food or wildflower. In ancient times, though, it was widely cultivated for its culinary and medicinal uses. The plant is native to the Mediterranean, but it has naturalized in the wild, growing freely throughout Europe and in large parts of Africa, North America, and Australia.

A WILD FOOD

Salsify is also known as oyster plant because its roots are described as having an oyster flavor and a mineral taste that evokes the sea. It is also commonly known as goatsbeard, Jerusalem star, and John-go-to-bed-at-noon (so called because its flowers close in the midday sun). Salsify roots are long and skinny, with creamy white flesh. They are cooked in much the same way as winter root vegetables, and can be added to soups and stews. They can also be consumed raw, shaved or grated in salads along with the edible leaves, flowers, and shoots. Young shoots can be steamed or braised as a fresh vegetable. Salsify belongs to the Asteraceae, or daisy family, and it produces purple, daisylike flowers on tall stems, followed by puffball seed heads. The plant self sows and spreads easily; in parts of Australia it is listed as an environmental weed.

Salsify flower and seed head

Helianthus tuberosus

SUNCHOKE

Sunchoke belongs to the Asteraceae, or daisy, aster, and sunflower family. It is a win-win plant, grown for its beautiful displays of sunflower-like blooms and for its knobby edible tubers. Other common names for this plant are Jerusalem artichoke, sunroot, and earth apple.

WHAT'S IN A NAME?

Sunchokes were first cultivated in precolonial times by Native Americans. Despite one of its confusing common names—Jerusalem artichoke—*Helianthus tuberosus* bears no relation to either Jerusalem or to artichokes. In 1605 the French explorer Samuel Champlain,

Sunchokes ready for the table

traveling in North America, described the tuber as having an artichoke flavor, and the name stuck. There is no single explanation for the reference to Jerusalem—most likely it is a corruption of the Italian word for sunflower, *girasole*. In the 1960s the vegetable was officially renamed and marketed as "sunchoke" in the United States. It is a high-yield, easy-to-grow plant with significant nutritional and health benefits.

Sunchoke in flower

Culinary Uses

The flavor of sunchoke is comparable to potato, but it is a little sweeter and has a crisp, juicy texture. The tubers are similar in appearance to ginger root. Unlike potatoes, sunchokes are palatable raw, with a texture similar to water chestnuts, and they can be shaved or sliced to add to salads. Sunchokes can also be stir-fried, steamed, boiled, roasted, puréed, and even made into chips. They are best eaten in simple preparations or lightly cooked so that their nutty flavor is not overwhelmed. Sunchokes in cream is a southern dish in which the tubers are boiled in their skins until just tender (this helps to preserve their texture and flavor). Then they are quickly peeled and added to a pan with a little butter and just enough heavy cream to coat the vegetables. The dish is seasoned with salt and black pepper.

Sunchokes in cream

Ipomoea batatas

SWEET POTATO

Sweet potato is a vigorous, heat-loving vine of the extended Convolvulaceae, or bindweed family. It is believed to have originated in Central or South America, and it has a long history as a cultivated food, reaching as far back as Polynesia in AD 700, and spreading from there to Japan and the Philippines.

Sweet potato tuber

ALL HAIL THE TATER

Sweet potato was a staple vegetable in the New World and an important vegetable in the United States until its popularity waned around the middle of the twentieth century. It is still grown extensively in the Southeast—it is the state vegetable of North Carolina, which leads in commercial production in the United States. Many parts of the South still hold annual festivals to celebrate the sweet potato. Tater Day, in Benton, Kentucky, was established in 1843 and continues today. Sweet potato is similar to the common potato in many ways, but they are not part of the same botanical family, and are only very distantly related. As the name indicates, sweet potato has a significantly higher sugar content and a sweeter flavor. They can be cooked like potatoes, or dried and ground into flour. Sweet potatoes are a nutrient-dense complex carbohydrate, rich in minerals and vitamins A, C, and B. Their flesh is typically a rich, orange hue, although there are purple, pink, red, and yellow varieties.

Characteristic orange flesh

Sweet potato flowers

CONTAINER GARDENING

The sweet potato plant has heart-shaped leaves and trumpet flowers that closely resemble those of bindweed or morning glory. It is an easy-to-grow, adaptable plant. Bush varieties will grow happily in containers, and will produce a modest harvest if adequate drainage and warmth are provided. Many cultivars of sweet potato have been developed solely for ornamental use; their foliage ranges from lime green to dark purple, and the leaves may be heart-shaped or deeply lobed.

Ornamental sweet potato in container

Colocasia esculenta

TARO

Taro is a moisture-loving tropical plant of the Araceae family, native to Southeast Asia. It is grown for its edible, starchy corms, or rhizomatous tubers, and also for use as an ornamental plant. It is commonly known as elephant ear for its oversized, heart-shaped leaves. Taro is widely cultivated as a staple vegetable throughout the West Indies, China, Japan, and Polynesia.

HAWAIIAN FAVORITE

The taro root (as it is commonly called) is a corm, shaped like a spinning top. The flavor and texture are similar to sweet potato or potato. All parts of the taro plant contain the toxic compound calcium oxalate, which is removed by cooking. Taro is a staple food in Hawaii, where it is used to make the traditional poi dish, a pastelike preparation of boiled and mashed taro mixed with water and flavorings. The leaves and young shoots of the plant are also edible. Taro thrives in wet, boggy soil, so it is well suited to streams and lakeside locations. The leaves reach two to three feet in length, and they grow on tall petioles that sprout directly from the corm. This plant adds drama and architectural interest to the garden, and many ornamental cultivars have been developed; however, the fast-growing, dense habit of the plant has earned it the status of invasive weed in parts of the United States and Hawaii.

Hawaiian poi dish

Cyperus esculentus

TIGERNUT

Also known as yellow nutsedge, earth almond, or *chufa* in Spanish, tigernut is a member of the sprawling Cyperaceae, or sedge family. It is an ancient plant that grows extensively as a weed across the globe, but it is also cultivated for its edible tubers.

Dried tigernuts

LAWN BAD, KITCHEN GOOD

Sedges and grasses are similar in appearance, the main distinguishing feature being the shape of the leaf stem; sedge stems are triangular in form, whereas grass stems are round. *Cyperus esculentus* is a vigorous plant with deep roots and brittle stems that break easily when pulled. It produces copious seeds, so eradicating this plant from the garden can be difficult. In many places the tigernut plant is considered a noxious weed, but its edible tubers are nutritious and palatable. The small tubers, or nutlets, are similar in shape and size to hazelnuts, and they have a sweet, nutty flavor akin to roasted chestnuts. Tigernuts are popular as a dried snack, used in cereals, or blended with water to make tigernut milk. Commercially available in dried form, tigernuts have a distinctive wrinkled appearance. Dried tigernuts are hard, so they are typically rehydrated before eating. They are an excellent substitute for nuts and flours in baked goods, and because they are tubers, not nuts, they are free of the common allergens associated with nuts, seeds, and grains.

Curcuma longa

TURMERIC

Aromatic turmeric is a member of the Zingiberaceae, or ginger family, and native to South Asia. Its culinary use dates back 4,000 years in India, and it has a long history as a medicinal and ceremonial plant. Turmeric is cultivated throughout tropical Asia, with India leading in commercial production.

COMPLEX AND SUBTLE FLAVOR

Turmeric's knobby tubers are eaten as a fresh vegetable or dried and ground into an aromatic powder. The tubers are boiled or steamed before use. Turmeric is an essential spice in South Asian and Middle Eastern cuisines, and is a key ingredient in most curry

Knobby turmeric roots

powders. It is also used to add color to foods such as rice and dairy products. The fresh root or the dried spice can be added to hearty soups, stews, and curries. Fresh turmeric root has a zesty flavor that is more subtle than the powder. It can be grated or julienned for use in coleslaws, puréed for soups, or pickled as chutney. The richly pigmented yellow color of raw turmeric comes from the active chemical curcumin. Turmeric has been used as a natural dye since 600 BC, and it lent the robes of Buddhist monks their distinctive orange color. The plant has glossy, oblong leaves, and it produces stunning pink, purple, or white flowers.

Turmeric flower

Medicinal Uses

Turmeric was used for centuries in the traditional medicines of India, China, Japan, and Egypt. Its historic medicinal uses are too many to list, but modern science has borne out the impressive healthful properties of the plant. Today turmeric is valued for its powerful antioxidant properties. Scientists believe it has anti-inflammatory, antimicrobial, antimutagenic, and anticancer actions. It continues to be closely studied in the modern scientific community, especially its possible benefits in the field of memory function, and in the search for treatments for Alzheimer's disease.

Turmeric powder

Brassica rapa ssp. *rapa*
TURNIP

The turnip has been cultivated since ancient times. It is a close relative of rutabaga, but typically smaller in size with white or pale yellow flesh. It is a hardy, cool-weather vegetable; warm weather produces a woody, tasteless crop. The turnip is a biennial plant, and it produces pretty yellow flowers on tall stems in its second year; in hot temperatures the plant may "bolt" and flower early.

Flowering turnip plant

BEST WHEN YOUNG

Turnips come in a variety of shapes and sizes. The type found in the average grocery store has two-toned purple and white skin, but there are also yellow, green, red, white, and numerous heirloom varieties. Turnips generally grow in a smooth, globular form, but they are also available in flattened globe, spindle, tapered, or egg-shaped varieties. They are harvested when they measure about two to three inches across because the flavor deteriorates as the plant matures. The flavor of turnip is less sweet than that of rutabaga, and more cabbagelike, with a hint of pepper. Turnip leaves are edible and highly nutritious, and turnip greens are especially popular in the southern United States.

Red and white turnip cultivars

Wasabia japonica

WASABI

Wasabi is a semiaquatic plant native to Japan. It is a member of the Brassicaceae family, which contains the similarly pungent plants mustard and horseradish. The stem of the wasabi plant is especially tangy, and it is widely used as a condiment and flavoring in Japanese cuisine.

Grating wasabi root

TRUE OR FALSE?

Wasabi is available in two qualities: the finest grade, *sawa wasabi*, can be found growing wild in the wet earth beside cold mountain streams; a less highly regarded type, *oka wasabi*, is grown in fields as a commercial crop. True wasabi, however, is relatively rare and very expensive; many wasabi pastes served in restaurants and sold in grocery stores contain very little or no actual wasabi. Instead, they are a horseradish-based imitation, dyed with green food coloring. Wasabi paste is made by grating wasabi root to a fine, smooth texture. Traditionally this was done using a sharkskin grater, but ceramic graters are a common substitute. Wasabi root is knobby and green. Fresh wasabi leaves are edible, and they have a similar spicy flavor. They are often used as a decorative garnish in Japanese dishes.

Wasabi-flavored peas

Eleocharis dulcis

WATER CHESTNUT

Not a nut, but definitely a water vegetable, *Eleocharis dulcis*, or Chinese water chestnut, is a tropical plant of the Cyperaceae family of sedges. The plant produces small, edible corms in the mud below shallow, slow-moving marshes, bogs, or paddy fields.

EXCEPTIONAL TEXTURE

Water chestnuts are closely associated with Chinese and Southeast Asian cuisines. They are served raw in salads, or are added to stir-fried dishes, soups, and curries. They are valued for their mild, sweet flavor and crunchy texture, which does not diminish during cooking. They can also be crystallized and pickled. In Asia, water chestnuts are enjoyed boiled, and blended or puréed and made into a mild- flavored drink.

Harvested water chestnuts

Peeled water chestnuts

Tab tim krob *dessert*

Culinary Uses

Red rubies in coconut milk is the enticing name of the popular Thai dessert *tab tim krob*—an essential treat in hot weather. It is a colorful dish that combines water chestnuts with coconut milk sweetened with sugar and flavored with pandanus leaves. The water chestnuts are dyed with red food coloring, dredged in tapioca flour, and boiled very briefly before being removed and plunged into cold water. This creates a candylike texture that is gelatinous on the outside and crunchy at the center. The cooled water chestnuts are placed in a serving dish with sweetened coconut milk and shaved or crushed ice.

Smallanthus sonchifolius
YACÓN

Yacón is a close relative of the sunflower and sunchoke, with a similar appearance and habit to the sunflower. It is an Andean crop grown for its edible rhizomes, or tubers, that are roughly the size of a potato. Their flavor is a palatable, slightly floral combination of celery, pear, and apple. Another common name for this vegetable is Peruvian ground apple. As might be surmised, the flesh of the yacón tuber is sweet, crisp, and juicy. It is eaten raw in salads, or boiled, roasted, and added to stews. Yacón can be pressed to make a sweet drink; in South America the juice is condensed to produce syrup.

Yacón flower and tubers

Dioscorea

YAM

The yam is the best-known species in the large, diverse Dioscoreaceae family. It is a tropical plant native to Africa, and it produces large, edible tubers. Yam is widely consumed around the world, with the bulk of production occuring in Africa.

SKIN-DEEP BEAUTY

Hundreds of varieties of cultivated and wild yam exist. None of them are much to look at on the outside, but underneath the rough outer skin, the smooth flesh of the yam is yellow, orange, white, or an attractive violet color. Yam is a high-fiber, starchy vegetable similar in texture and flavor to sweet potato, and it is used in both savory and sweet dishes. Yam can be baked, boiled, fried, mashed, or pounded into a paste. White and yellow yams are the most widely cultivated. In the Philippines, purple yam *(Dioscorea alata)*, known as *ube*, is used to create ice cream, confectionaries, and cakes of a vivid purple hue. Yam is widely grown in China as a food and for use in traditional

Purple yam

Filipino ube cake made with purple yam

medicine. Its Chinese name, *shan yao*, translates as "mountain medicine." Another species of yam native to tropical Asia is *Dioscorea bulbifera*, commonly known as air potato. It is not widely cultivated, but it is valued as a high-yield—but also highly invasive—garden vegetable. It grows extremely rapidly and produces potato-size bulbils on leaf stems high above the ground.

Air potato

Arracacia xanthorrhiza

Arracacha

Arracacha's texture, flavor, and appearance are very close to those of yam and it is often used as a substitute when yam is not available. Like yam, arracacha's stout conical roots come in a variety of white, orange, or purple hues. Arracacha is grown mainly in South America, where it has numerous common names, including little cassava, white carrot, and Creole celery. Its English name is Peruvian parsnip. In Brazil it is an important food crop widely cultivated for commercial production.

GENTLE ON THE STOMACH

Arracacha is prepared in much the same way as yam, and it can also be processed as flour. It is easily digested, so it is a good choice for people with delicate digestive systems, and it is often used in baby food. Arracacha is high in calcium—containing four times as much as the potato—and vitamin A. Like yam, arracacha is grown primarily for its starchy root, but its young leaves and stems also can be eaten like celery. The raw flavor of arracacha is described as a blend of carrot and celeriac (it is a member of the Apiaceae, or carrot family). When cooked, arracacha develops a mild, nutty flavor with a hint of roast chestnut. Arracacha chips are a popular Andean snack. The plant is slow to mature, taking up to eighteen months before it is ready to be harvested.

Colorful arracacha varieties

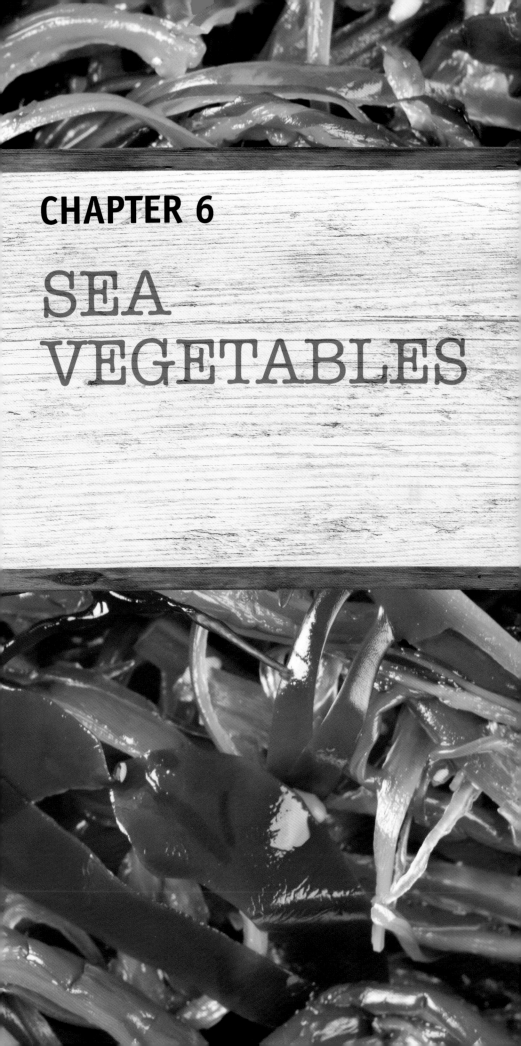

CHAPTER 6

SEA
VEGETABLES

Monostroma

AONORI

Aonori is a species of green seaweed belonging to the Monostromataceae family. It is a monostromatic seaweed, which means it has a single layer of cells spread across very thin, leaflike membranes.

COLORFUL TOPPING

This seaweed is found growing in rock pools and shallow seawater in the bays and gulfs in southern Japan. It is also known as green laver, and it is a relative of laver found in the cold waters of Britain and Ireland. In Japan, aonori is extensively cultivated for commercial use by growing it in deeper waters on seaweed nets attached to floating rafts. Aonori is marketed in dried form, finely flaked or powdered. It is used as a confetti-like topping for foods such as sushi, or as a flavoring ingredient in soups and other hot dishes. It imparts a delicate, grassy seaweed flavor and a distinctive aroma, and it is also valued for its rich green color. Aonori is a nutrient-dense food, high in protein and rich in vitamins, minerals, and amino acids.

Aonori seaweed farm

French fries dusted with aonori flakes

Eisenia bicyclis
ARAME

Eisenia bicyclis is a species of edible kelp belonging to the Lessoniaceae, or kelp family, of algae. It is native to the temperate waters of the Pacific Ocean around Japan, and it is also widely cultivated in South Korea. Most often it is called arame, and another common name is sea oak.

LITTLE KELP

Kelp is a large, fast-growing seaweed that can reach up to 250 feet in length, and can form vast underwater forests. Arame is a small species of kelp that grows to only three feet in length. It produces many brown, feathery, flat blades (thalli) from a thin woody stipe, or stem, that attaches to rocks below the water. Arame is handpicked by divers or mechanically harvested, and it is used extensively in Asian cuisines. It is generally sold shredded and dried, and is rehydrated before cooking. Dried arame is dark brown with a finely threaded form.

Shredded arame

It has a mild, sweet flavor and firm texture that is adaptable to many kinds of dishes. It may be finely chopped and served raw in salads, or it can be steamed, boiled, or fried, or added to soups and stews. It is a high-fiber, high-protein food, rich in minerals, calcium, and vitamin A. Extract of arame has been found to have anti-inflammatory properties, and it is highly regarded as a gentle detoxifier.

Dish with arame

Chondrus crispus

CARRAGEEN MOSS

Carrageen moss is a small seaweed with a branching form that belongs to the Gigartinaceae red algae family. Its name is derived from the Irish word *carraigín*, which means "moss of the rock" or "little rock." It can be found growing along the Irish coastline and in parts of Europe and North America that meet the cold waters of the Atlantic ocean.

GELATIN ACTION

Carrageen moss contains a hydrocolloid called carrageenan, which is a natural gelling agent used to stabilize, emulsify, and improve the texture of many foods. It has a wide range of applications in the food industry and also in traditional Irish cuisine, where it is used in both savory and sweet dishes. Carrageen moss is used to make a creamy dessert called carrageen moss blancmange (or pudding). The hydrocolloids in the seaweed have a gelatinlike action, setting the pudding as it cools. In Ireland sweetened extract of carrageen moss was also used as a traditional medicine to soothe a sore throat and ease the symptoms of a cold. Like all seaweeds, carrageen moss is a nutrient-dense food. This species is rich in vitamins A, K, E; essential fatty acids omega 3 and omega 6; and the minerals calcium, potassium, and sulfur. It also contains iodine, which supports healthy thyroid function.

Carrageen moss blancmange

Alaria esculenta

DABBERLOCKS

Commonly known by the picturesque name dabberlocks, *Alaria esculenta* is a seaweed of the Alariaceae family of kelp. Among the many other names for this algae are badderlocks, winged kelp, Irish wakame, Atlantic wakame, murlins, and honeyware. In Ireland it is called *láir* or *láracha*.

TENACIOUS GRIP

Dabberlocks is native to the cold, rough waters of the North Atlantic. It is a common seaweed found growing along the North Atlantic coast, the North Sea, and the North Pacific. It grows prolifically in rocky, shallow waters, and it produces long, feather-shaped fronds (its Latin name, *Alaria esculenta*, loosely translates as "edible wings"). The yellow-brown fronds typically grow up to six feet in length, and they are tough and flexible. By means of a strong, rootlike structure called a holdfast, they are able to anchor themselves firmly to the rocks and withstand intense battering from the waves. Raw or cooked fresh, dabberlocks have a long culinary history among the peoples of Britain, Ireland, Greenland, and Iceland. Its high levels of vitamin A means that it also has a wide application in skin creams and lotions. Dabberlocks contains the vitamins K, C, B2, B6, and B12, and several essential minerals.

Rocky North Atlantic coastline

Palmaria palmata
DULSE

This attractive, blood-red seaweed is a Rhodophyta algae—an extremely ancient and large group of algae containing thousands of species. Other common English names are dillisk, sea kale, and sea parsley. Dulse shares the same geographical spread as dabberlocks, reaching from the North Atlantic coast and North Sea to the North Pacific. In parts of Europe, it has been cultivated as food for over a thousand years.

SEEING RED

Red algae obtain their nutrients through photosynthesis, and they contain the photosynthetic pigments phycoerythrins. These pigments absorb blue and green light while reflecting red light, concealing other pigments so that the algae appear only to be red. Dulse produces wide, leathery

Dulse, pickled beets, and kale salad

ribbons up to twenty inches long. It has a slightly nutty flavor and can be served raw as a snack, cooked in broths and stews, or baked in cakes and breads. It is also marketed in dried form to be used as seasoning. Dulse can be extracted as an herbal supplement, and it is a popular ingredient in skin creams and gels. While the widespread use of dulse as a modern food has waned, it is still popular in Iceland (where it is called *söl*). In the small coastal town of Ballycastle in the far north of Ireland, dulse is still served at the Ould Lammas Fair, a harvest festival dating back to 1612.

Saccharina japonica

KOMBU

This seaweed belongs to the Laminariaceae family of kelps, and it is native to Japan. It is a commercially important sea crop, cultivated

extensively throughout Asia. Kombu is one of the most widely consumed seaweeds in Japan, China, and Korea.

CULTIVATING KOMBU

Kombu produces long, bladelike fronds that can reach over thirty feet in length. They are tethered to rocks far below the water surface by a strong holdfast, or rootlike anchor. Today only a third of kombu eaten is harvested from naturally occurring seabeds. Demand for the kelp has led to large-scale artificial cultivation. Commercial production of kombu is done in a series of steps. Spores from the seaweed are germinated in specially cooled nursery tanks enriched with fertilizers. Once the tiny sporelings are established, they are transferred to long ropes, and then moved out to the ocean to mature. They are harvested when they reach around six feet in length. The ropes are held afloat by buoys, tethered at each end to the seabed. The crop is harvested by hand, dried, and marketed in sheets. Kombu is rehydrated before cooking. Its flavor permeates much of Asian cuisine, as it is frequently used to make *dashi*, a seaweed stock that forms the basis for soups and stews. Kombu is generally used to impart flavor to other foods, and it may be pickled and wrapped around fish, like in the popular dish *kombu maki*.

Sheets of dried kombu

Porphyra umbilicalis

LAVER

Laver is a species of cold-water purple algae of the *Porphyra* genus, which grows along the shores of Britain, Ireland, and other parts of the North Atlantic coastline.

Other species of *Porphyra* are extensively cultivated in Asia, primarily *Pyropia yezeonensis*, which is called *nori* in Japan, *zicai* in China, and *gim* in Korea. Laver has been cultivated in Asia since the seventeenth century; today China leads the world in commercial production.

Culinary Uses

In Japan, nori is a familiar food used primarily in sushi preparations. It is sold dried in wafer-thin sheets, with the delicate consistency of rice paper. In Britain and Ireland, laver was a forage food for centuries, where it is also known as kelp or slake. In Wales laver is still used to make a traditional bread called *bara lawr*. Laver is a food of great historical importance to the Welsh. It could be freely harvested and used as a subsistence food in times of crisis. The first written records of it date back to 1607. In the eighteenth century, laver bread was a staple food among the Welsh mining community, providing a low-cost, high-energy source of nutrition for men working in the coal mines, and it remains an integral part of the Welsh diet. Laver grows clinging to the rocks in shallow waters in the intertidal zone. It is harvested at low tide and air-dried on laver huts. To make laver bread, the seaweed is washed, boiled, and pulped into a dark paste. It is generally served with meat dishes, and it may be mixed with oats and formed into patties.

Laver bread

Cladosiphon okamuranus

MOZUKU

This brown algae is a popular edible seaweed native to Okinawa in Japan. It is mildly flavored with a slimy consistency, and it is enjoyed for its stringy texture. Mozuku is usually eaten cold as a salad or as a side dish, and it is offset with vinegar. It is available in dried form, and is reconstituted before cooking.

Mozuku salad

Medicinal Uses

Mozuku is highly regarded for its nutritional and health benefits. It is a low-calorie, high-fiber, nutrient-dense food that contains the highest levels of the phytochemical fucoidan out of all the brown seaweeds. Preliminary research into this compound has shown that fucoidan has antiviral, antitumor, anticarcinogen, and anti-inflammatory actions. This gives it great potential as a health supplement, and as a useful compound in the search for anticancer pharmaceuticals.

Fucoidan also promotes healthy blood cells. Brown seaweeds have traditionally been used as treatments for high blood pressure. The anticoagulant action in fucoidan is believed to be helpful in preventing blood clots.

Powdered mozuku

Gracilaria

OGONORI

Ogonori is a pretty, edible red seaweed also known as ogo, and sea moss. It is widely consumed in Southeast Asia, Hawaii, and the Caribbean. The mucilaginous properties of this seaweed are used to make the algae-based gelatin agar.

Ogonori is served fresh in salads, and is often used as a garnish for *sashimi*. It is a low-calorie, high-fiber food, and is a good source of vitamin K and manganese.

The *Gracilaria* species of red seaweed is also cultivated for ornamental use in aquariums.

Red ogonori seaweed

SEA VEGETABLE GALLERY

Seaweeds and sea vegetables provide abundant nutrition and are among the world's healthiest foods. Edible algae are divided into red, green, and brown color groups.

1

2

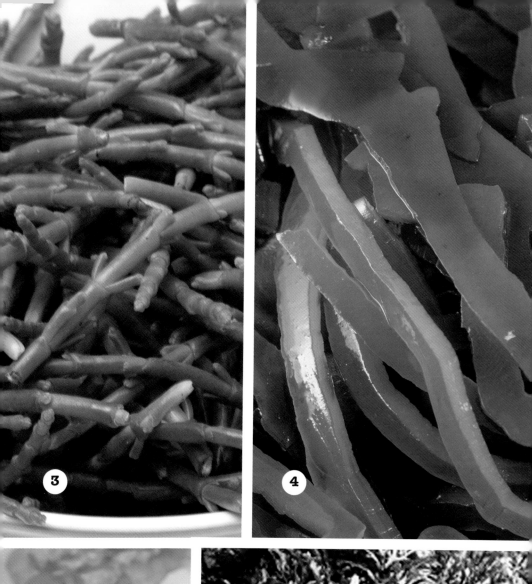

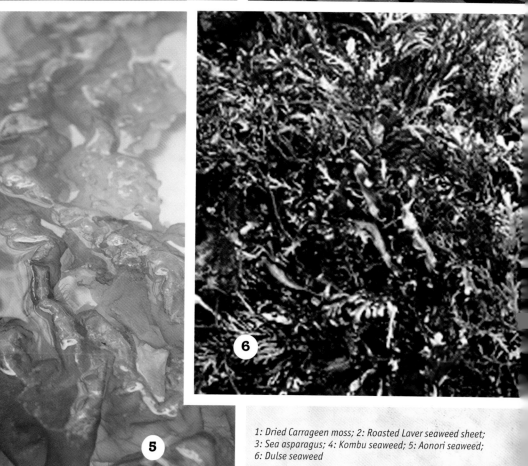

1: Dried Carrageen moss; 2: Roasted Laver seaweed sheet;
3: Sea asparagus; 4: Kombu seaweed; 5: Aonori seaweed;
6: Dulse seaweed

Salicornia europaea

SEA ASPARAGUS

Unlike seaweed, which is an algae, sea asparagus is an edible halophyte, a salt-tolerant plant of the *Salicornia* genus. It grows in the salt marshes, beaches, and tidal mudflats of northwest Europe. As few as 2 percent of plants can survive in salty conditions.

A FISHERMAN'S VEGETABLE

Sea asparagus has a long culinary history in England, where it is typically known as samphire. Other regional names include glasswort, sea pickle, pickleweed, sampkin, sampha, and marsh samphire. The word "samphire" is a corruption of the French name for the

Sea asparagus

vegetable, *herbe de Saint-Pierre*. Saint Peter is the patron saint of fishermen. Sea asparagus grows on wave-battered, rocky outcrops, and some species grow on steep cliffs, so harvesting the plant can be hazardous. It is gathered when young and served as a fresh or pickled vegetable. Once commonly consumed throughout coastal England, today it may be offered on the menus of fine restaurants as a special treat. Its common name, glasswort, reveals a surprising additional use for the plant—in medieval England, ashes from burned plants were fused with sand in the production of glass.

Culinary Uses

Sea asparagus can be cooked in much the same ways as asparagus, but it does not have an asparagus flavor. It has a salty taste that evokes the sea, so it is a natural accompaniment to fish or seafood. Steamed sea asparagus is typically served with melted butter, but unlike asparagus, it is best soaked beforehand, and it is not necessary to season it with salt. The razor-thin, segmented spears require very little cooking. They are added to soups and stews at the last minute, or stir-fried. The plant has tender, succulent flesh with a woody core that is easily removed.

Sea asparagus with halibut

Steamed sea asparagus

Ulva lactuca

SEA LETTUCE

Sea lettuce is a common edible green seaweed that can be found growing in calm intertidal waters and sheltered coastlines all over the world.

It is in the Chlorophyta division of algae, and it acquires nutrients from its surroundings.

ENVIRONMENTAL GAUGE

The broad, ruffled fronds of sea lettuce are fine and translucent, only two cells thick. As a food it has a delicate texture, mild flavor, and distinctive aroma of the sea. Underwater, this seaweed looks much like a vivid, green Boston bib lettuce; at low tide it can cover rocks and beaches with a dense layer of dark green slime. If provided with surplus nutrients from agricultural runoff or pollution, sea lettuce can form large blooms that range from a smelly nuisance to a serious health hazard, as it emits methane, hydrogen sulfide, and other noxious gases as it decomposes. The levels of sea lettuce can be used as an indicator of pollution, and it is advisable when buying sea lettuce for food to check the source. Sea lettuce can also tolerate brackish waters, and it may be found growing in estuaries and marshes.

Sea lettuce

Undaria pinnatifida
WAKAME

Wakame grows in the temperate waters of the Pacific, Indian, and Atlantic Oceans. It is an adaptable seaweed, often found growing on buoys and other marine structures. Cultivated in Japan and Korea for centuries, wakame is a staple food among East Asian populations.

FREE DIVING TRADITION

This seaweed develops single, ruffled blades up to nine feet long on thick stipes with a tough holdfast at the base. For around 2,000 years female Japanese divers, known as *ama*, have harvested seaweed without breathing apparatus, diving in deep waters to cut the wakame directly from the seabed. Wakame has a smooth, slippery texture and a sweet, briny flavor. It is served raw as a salad, and is used in numerous soups and stews, notably in the ubiquitous *miso* soup, a Japanese light soup with a distinctive aroma. In Korea, wakame is used in a seaweed-laden soup called *miyeokguk*.

Both these soups are highly nutritious, and because of their elevated levels of calcium and iodine, they are heavily consumed by pregnant women and nursing mothers. *Miyeokguk* is also a traditional birthday food, given to children to remind them of the first nourishment they received in life from their mother.

Miyeokguk soup

CHAPTER 7

RECIPES

Sides, Salads & Soups
Mains
Sauces & Pickles

Sides, Salads & Soups

Arugula with Warm Beets & Goat Cheese

Serves 6 as a side dish

6 medium beets, washed, tops removed
½ cup balsamic vinegar
½ cup extra virgin olive oil
2 teaspoons Dijon mustard
Salt and freshly ground black pepper
3½ cups baby arugula
½ cup pine nuts, toasted
½ cup goat cheese, crumbled

1. Preheat the oven to 400°F.
2. Wrap each beet in aluminum foil and place them on a baking tray. Roast for 50 minutes to 1 hour, until tender.
3. Whisk together the vinegar, olive oil, mustard, 2 teaspoons salt, and 1 teaspoon pepper and set aside.
4. When the beets are cooked, remove from the oven, unwrap, and allow to cool slightly.
5. Cut the beets into medium-sized wedges and then stir them into a bowl containing half of the vinaigrette, 1 teaspoon salt, and ¼ teaspoon pepper.
6. Place the arugula on a serving plate, and arrange the beets, almonds, and goat cheese on top. Drizzle with vinaigrette, season with salt and pepper, and serve warm.

Baked Onions with Thyme

Serves 6 as a side dish

6 medium onions, peeled and halved
2 tablespoons extra virgin olive oil
¼ cup balsamic vinegar
2 teaspoons dark brown sugar
1 tablespoon fresh thyme
Salt and freshly ground black pepper

1. Preheat the oven to 350°F.
2. In a large bowl combine the onions, olive oil, vinegar, and brown sugar, and stir until onions are well coated.
3. Place the mixture in a large baking dish, sprinkle on the thyme, and season well with salt and pepper.
4. Cover with foil and cook for 25 minutes.
5. Remove and discard the foil, stir the onions, and return to the oven for 20–25 minutes until golden and tender. Serve immediately.

Braised Asparagus & Celery with Shallots

Serves 6 as a side dish

1 pound asparagus, tough ends removed
4 medium-length celery stalks, trimmed
1 tablespoon extra virgin olive oil
2 large shallots, peeled and chopped
2 tablespoons water
2 tablespoons sliced almonds, toasted
Salt and freshly ground black pepper

1. Cut the asparagus and celery stalks into 2-inch lengths.
2. In a 10-inch skillet, heat the oil over medium heat, and fry the shallots for 3 minutes.
3. Add the water, asparagus, and celery, cover and cook, stirring occasionally, for 10 minutes.
4. Drain the vegetables, combine with the toasted almonds, and season well.

Citrus Spring Greens

Serves 4 as a side dish

Zest of 1 lemon
Juice of ½ lemon
2 tablespoons extra virgin olive oil
Salt and freshly ground black pepper
1 pound spring greens, such as collard greens or curly kale, stalks trimmed

1. Combine the lemon zest and the juice in a small jar.
2. Add the olive oil with a tiny pinch of salt and pepper. Put the lid securely on the jar and shake well.
3. Bring to a boil a large saucepan half-filled with cold water and a pinch of salt.
4. Cut the spring greens in half lengthwise, then finely slice them.
5. Add the spring greens to the boiling water and cook for 3–4 minutes, or until tender but still retaining color.
6. Drain the spring greens, shake off excess water, then tip back into the pan.
7. Give the dressing another good shake, then drizzle over the greens.
8. Toss the spring greens in the dressing while they're still hot, then transfer to a serving dish and serve immediately.

Fennel & Onion Soup

Serves 4–6

½ cup unsalted butter
¼ cup extra virgin olive oil
3 pounds mild onions, thickly sliced
2 pounds fennel, tops and cores removed,
    sliced ¼ inch thick
½ cup each dry sherry and Cognac
1½ cups dry white wine
8 cups beef stock
3 bay leaves
1 tablespoon kosher salt
1½ teaspoons freshly ground black pepper
1 small loaf of sourdough bread, crusts
    removed, thickly sliced, and toasted
1–1½ cups Gruyère cheese, grated

1. Heat the butter and oil in a large heavy-
bottomed pan over medium–high heat, add
the onions and fennel, and cook for 30–40
minutes, stirring occasionally, until the
onions turn a rich, golden brown.
2. Add the sherry and Cognac, scraping
up the brown bits in the pan, and simmer
uncovered for 5 minutes.
3. Add the white wine and simmer
uncovered for another 15 minutes.
4. Add the beef stock, bay leaves, salt, and
pepper, bring to a boil, lower the heat, and
simmer uncovered for 20 minutes. Remove
the bay leaves and season to taste.
5. Preheat the broiler. Ladle the soup into
ovenproof serving bowls, top with the toasted
bread, sprinkle with the grated Gruyère,
and broil for 3–5 minutes, 5 inches below
the heat source, until the cheese is melted
and bubbly. Serve immediately.

Fragrant Ginger Rice

Serves 4 as a side dish

1 tablespoon olive oil
1 onion, sliced
2 cloves garlic, crushed
¼ inch ginger root, finely chopped
1 generous cup long-grain rice
1 cup button mushrooms, sliced
2 cups hot vegetable stock
½ teaspoon ground turmeric
2 tablespoons chopped fresh cilantro
Salt and freshly ground black pepper

1. In a pan, heat the oil and cook the onion,
garlic, and ginger for 5 minutes until golden.
2. Add the rice and cook, stirring, for 1
minute. Add mushrooms, vegetable stock,
and turmeric, then bring to a boil.
3. Cover and simmer until the liquid
is absorbed and the rice is tender,
approximately 15–20 minutes.
4. Stir in the cilantro, season with salt
and pepper, and serve immediately.

Garlic Mashed Potatoes

Serves 6 as a side dish

1 cup extra virgin olive oil
½ cup garlic cloves, peeled
3 pounds Yukon Gold potatoes, peeled
    and quartered
Salt
1 teaspoon freshly ground black pepper
¼ cup heavy cream, half-and-half, or
    sour cream

1. Heat the oil and garlic in a small pan,
bring to a boil, then turn the heat to low and
cook uncovered until the garlic is lightly
browned. Turn off the heat and set aside;
the garlic will continue to cook in the oil.
2. Place the potatoes in a large pot of salted
water, bring to a boil, and cook for 15–20
minutes, until the potatoes are very tender.
3. Remove the potatoes from the water,
reserving the cooking water, and remove the
garlic from the oil, reserving the oil.
4. Process the potatoes and garlic in a food
processor fitted with the medium disk. Add
the reserved olive oil, 2 teaspoons of salt, the
pepper, cream, and ¾ cup of the cooking
water to the potatoes, and mix with a wooden
spoon until the potatoes are creamy but still
firm. If necessary, add more cooking water.
5. Season to taste, and serve immediately.

Gazpacho

Serves 6 as a side dish

2 (28-ounce) cans whole peeled tomatoes,
    drained
4 scallions
¼ seedless cucumber, or seeds removed
1 large red onion
6 garlic cloves
½ cup red wine vinegar
½ cup extra virgin olive oil, plus extra
    for croutons and drizzling
½ teaspoon celery salt
¼ teaspoon crushed red pepper flakes
2 tablespoons tomato paste
1½ cups tomato juice
1 tablespoon salt
1½ teaspoons freshly ground black pepper

1. Cut the tomatoes, scallions, cucumber,
and onion in large pieces.
2. Place the vegetables and garlic in a food
processor fitted with the steel blade and
pulse until the soup is coarsely puréed.
3. Place the mixture in a large bowl and
whisk in all other ingredients.
4. Cover with plastic wrap and chill for
4 hours or overnight.
5. Serve topped with Herby Goat Croutons,
page 273.

Herby Goat Croutons

(Accompanies Gazpacho Soup, page 272)

1 baguette
Olive oil
1/2 cup garlic and herb goat cheese

1. Preheat the broiler.
2. Cut 6 thick, diagonal slices from the baguette. Place on a sheet pan, brush with olive oil, and broil for 1–2 minutes, 5 to 7 inches from the heat.
3. Turn the slices, spread with the goat cheese, and broil for another minute, until the cheese is warm and the bread is toasted.
4. Serve the warm goat cheese croutons with bowls of cold Gazpacho, page 272.

Herb-Roasted Roots

Serves 8–10 as a side dish

2 cups acorn or butternut squash, peeled, deseeded, and cut into 1/2-inch pieces
2 cups each waxy potatoes, (such as King Edward or Yukon Gold), carrots, celeriac, parsnips, and turnips, peeled and cut into 1/2-inch pieces
3/4 cup extra virgin olive oil
Salt and freshly ground black pepper
4 cloves chopped garlic
6 sprigs each fresh rosemary and thyme

1. Preheat the oven to 400°F.
2. Place the vegetables on a sheet pan, and drizzle with the olive oil.
3. Season with salt and pepper, and mix until the vegetables are well-coated.
4. Spread out in a single layer, roast for 30 minutes, turning once during cooking.
5. Stir in the garlic, rosemary, and thyme. Roast for another 10–15 minutes, until the vegetables are tender and starting to brown.
6. Serve immediately.

Lemongrass & Leek Soup

Serves 6

1/4 cup extra virgin olive oil
3 cloves garlic, chopped
6 stems lemongrass, finely sliced
3 pounds leeks, trimmed, washed, and finely sliced
2 large potatoes, peeled and parboiled
6 cups chicken or vegetable stock
Salt and freshly ground black pepper

1. Heat the oil in a large pan, add garlic and lemongrass, and fry gently for 3–4 minutes.
2. Add the leeks and potatoes, cook for 8 minutes, then add the stock, season, and cook until the vegetables are soft.
3. Liquidize until very smooth, reheat, and serve immediately.

Minestrone Soup

Serves 6

10 large ripe plum tomatoes, or 2 (14-ounce) cans of tomatoes, drained
1 tablespoon extra virgin olive oil
3 carrots, peeled and chopped
2 leeks, outer leaves removed, chopped
5 stalks celery, chopped
2 red onions, chopped
2 cloves garlic, finely sliced
1 heaped tablespoon chopped rosemary
3 cups chicken, or vegetable stock
3 cups baby spinach
3 handfuls basil, torn
2 cups small pasta shells
Salt and freshly ground black pepper
Grated Parmesan cheese

1. If using fresh tomatoes, place tomatoes in boiling water for 1 minute to loosen skins. Remove from water, then peel off the skins. Remove seeds, and roughly dice.
2. Warm a heavy-bottomed pan over medium heat, and add carrots, leeks, celery, onion, garlic, and rosemary. Cook until just tender, about for 15 minutes.
3. Add tomatoes and cook for 2 minutes, then add stock, bring to a boil, and simmer for 15 minutes.
4. Add the pasta, and simmer for 5 more minutes or until the pasta is just tender.
5. Stir in the spinach and basil leaves.
6. Season with salt and pepper, and serve immediately with grated Parmesan.

Potatoes Boulangère

Serves 6–8 as a side dish

9 medium Desirée or Red Bliss potatoes, peeled and very thinly sliced
2 medium onions, peeled, halved, and thinly sliced
Leaves from a few sprigs of fresh thyme
Salt and freshly ground black pepper
1 3/4 cups vegetable or chicken stock
1/2 cup butter

1. Preheat the oven to 350°F.
2. Butter an ovenproof dish approximately 12 inches x 8 inches x 2 inches deep.
3. Arrange in alternate layers the sliced potatoes, sliced onions, and a sprinkling of thyme, salt, and pepper. Finish with a layer of potatoes.
4. Pour the stock over the top, season with more salt, pepper, and thyme. Add small knobs of butter, dotted all over the top.
5. Place the dish on the top shelf of the oven and cook for an hour, or until the potatoes are tender and the top is crisp and golden.
6. Serve immediately.

Puréed Root Vegetables

Serves 4–6 as a side dish

2 cups each celeriac, parsnips, and starchy
   potatoes (such as Russets), peeled and
   cut into ½-inch pieces
4 tablespoons whole milk
2 tablespoons butter
Salt and freshly ground black pepper

1. Cook the celeriac, parsnips, and potatoes
in a large pan of boiling, salted water for
15 minutes until tender.
2. Drain and mash thoroughly, adding the
milk and butter as you mash.
3. Whisk until smooth with an electric
whisk, season, and serve immediately.

Roasted Spicy Bell Peppers

Serves 6 as a side dish

6 different colored bell peppers
¼ cup red wine vinegar
2 cloves garlic, minced
1 small hot chili, finely chopped
1 tablespoon capers, roughly chopped
2 tablespoons extra virgin olive oil
2 tablespoons fresh parsley, finely chopped
Salt and freshly ground black pepper

1. Preheat oven to 400°F.
2. Core, deseed, and halve the peppers.
3. Roast the peppers, skin upward, for
20–30 minutes.
4. Seal the peppers in a ziplock bag for 15
minutes.
5. Remove from the bag, peel the skins off
the peppers, and cut them into strips.
6. Combine all other ingredients in a large
bowl, stir in the peppers, and put aside to
marinate for several hours before serving.

Red Cabbage Braised with Garlic & Spices

Serves 8 as a side dish

2 pounds red cabbage, outer leaves removed
Salt and freshly ground black pepper
4 large tart apples, peeled, cored, and
   chopped small
4 large onions, peeled and chopped small
2 garlic cloves, finely chopped
1 teaspoon ground cinnamon
1 teaspoon ground nutmeg
½ teaspoon ground cloves
4 tablespoons soft brown sugar
3 tablespoons red wine vinegar
1–2 tablespoons butter

1. Preheat the oven to 320°F.
2. Quarter the cabbage, remove the central
stalk. Shred the cabbage finely.
3. In a large, ovenproof casserole place the
ingredients in alternate layers as follows:
cabbage sprinkled with salt and pepper,
and apples and onions sprinkled with
garlic, spices, and sugar.
4. Once all the ingredients are used, pour
over the red wine vinegar, and add knobs
of butter all over the top.
5. Cover with a tight-fitting lid and cook
in the oven for 2–2½ hours.

Roasted Tomato Caprese

Serves 6

12 plum tomatoes, halved lengthwise, seeds
   removed, but cores intact
¼ cup extra virgin olive oil, plus extra for
   drizzling
1½ tablespoons balsamic vinegar
2 large garlic cloves, minced
2 teaspoons sugar
Sea salt and freshly ground black pepper
16-ounce ball of fresh salted mozzarella
12 large fresh basil leaves

1. Preheat the oven to 275°F.
2. Arrange the tomatoes in a single layer
on a sheet pan, cut sides facing up, drizzle
with olive oil and balsamic vinegar, and
sprinkle with garlic, sugar, 1½ teaspoons
salt, and ½ teaspoon pepper.
3. Roast for 2 hours until the tomatoes
begin to caramelize, then remove from oven.
4. Cut the mozzarella into slices a little
under ½ inch thick.
5. Layer the tomatoes with the mozzarella
on a serving plate. Arrange the basil leaves
on top, sprinkle lightly with salt and
pepper, and drizzle with olive oil.
6. Serve immediately.

Rutabaga & Carrot Gratin

Serves 4–6 as a side dish

3 cups each rutabaga and carrots, peeled
   and cut into 1-inch pieces.
Salt and freshly ground black pepper
½–1 teaspoon grated nutmeg
1 cup grated strong-flavor cheese

1. Cook the rutabaga and carrots in a large
pan of boiling, salted water for 15 minutes.
2. Drain, season with salt, pepper, and
nutmeg, and mash thoroughly.
3. Put the mashed vegetables into an
ovenproof dish and sprinkle the cheese on top.
4. Finish under a broiler or in a preheated
oven until the cheese topping is golden
brown.
5. Serve immediately.

Sautéed Asparagus with Garlic and Chili

Serves 4 as a side dish

1/4 cup butter
2 tablespoons extra virgin olive oil
1 teaspoon each sea salt and freshly
   ground black pepper
3 cloves garlic, minced
Pinch of chili flakes or 1 fresh chili, chopped
1 pound fresh asparagus, trimmed

1. Melt the butter in a skillet over medium-high heat.
2. Stir in the olive oil, salt, pepper, garlic, and chili flakes and cook for 1 minute.
3. Add asparagus and cook, turning frequently, for 10 minutes.
4. Serve immediately.

Savory Lentils

Serves 4 as a side dish

3/4 cup green lentils
1/4 cup olive oil
1/2 cup diced onions
1/4 cup each carrot, celery, bell pepper, and
   green beans, chopped small
1 garlic clove, minced
1 garlic clove, halved*
1 tablespoon tomato paste
2 bay leaves
1 1/2 cups dry red wine
1 teaspoon Dijon mustard
Sea salt and freshly ground pepper
1 big bunch of spinach leaves, chopped
1 tablespoon butter or walnut oil
4 slices dense country bread*

1. Parboil the lentils for 5 minutes. Drain.
2. Heat 1 tablespoon of the oil in a large saucepan. Add the diced vegetables and cook over medium-high heat for a few minutes to brown them a bit.
3. Add the minced garlic, tomato paste, and the bay leaves, pour in the wine, and stir in the mustard.
4. Add 1 1/2 cups water, the lentils, and 1 teaspoon salt. Cover and simmer until the lentils are soft, 30-40 minutes.
5. Wash the spinach and wilt in a skillet with no additional water. Season with salt and pepper.
6. Stir the cooked greens into the lentils, and add a tablespoon of butter or walnut oil.
7. Season to taste and serve immediately.

* VARIATION:
For a light meal, toast the country bread and rub with the halved garlic. Cut each slice into quarters, arrange them on plates, and spoon lentils over the toast.

Spicy Potato Wedges

Serves 8 as a side dish

2 large sweet potatoes
2 medium potatoes
Sea salt and freshly ground black pepper
2 teaspoons sweet paprika
1 teaspoon chili powder
Olive oil

1. Preheat the oven to 400ºF.
2. Scrub the potatoes under cold running water.
3. Cut each potato in half lengthwise, and each half in half lengthwise again, and then each piece in half again to make 8 wedges.
4. Place the wedges in a large mixing bowl, season with salt and pepper, and sprinkle on the paprika and chili powder.
5. Drizzle over 2 tablespoons olive oil and stir everything together.
6. Spread out as a single layer on 2 large baking trays, and bake in the oven for 35-40 minutes, until golden brown and cooked through.
7. Remove the trays from the oven, leave to rest for 2-3 minutes, then transfer the potato wedges to a serving dish.

String Beans with Shallots

Serves 8 as a side dish

1 pound French* string beans, trimmed
Sea salt
2 tablespoons unsalted butter
1 tablespoon extra virgin olive oil
3 large shallots, diced in large pieces
1/2 teaspoon freshly ground black pepper

1. Blanch the beans in a large pot of boiling salted water for 1 1/2 minutes. Drain immediately and immerse in a bowl of ice water.
2. Heat the butter and oil in a very large sauté pan (12-inch diameter) or large pot.
3. Sauté the shallots on medium heat for 5-10 minutes, stirring occasionally, until lightly browned.
4. Drain the string beans and add to the shallots, mixing well. Heat until the beans are warmed through.
5. Season with 1/2 teaspoon salt and the pepper, and serve immediately.

* If using regular string beans, blanch for 2-3 minutes before using.

Sublime Glazed Carrots

Serves 8 as a side dish

2 large bunches of carrots,
    (approximately 2 pounds)
3 tablespoons butter
6 cloves of garlic, minced
1/4 cup superfine sugar
1 heaped tablespoon soft brown sugar
Juice of 2 clementines
1/2 bunch of fresh thyme
Salt and freshly ground black pepper

1. Trim and peel the carrots.
2. Melt the butter in a large skillet over medium heat.
3. Add the garlic with the sugars, clementine juice, and thyme, stir to combine all ingredients.
4. Lay the carrots in the bottom of the pan, season well, cover, and reduce to low heat.
5. Cook until the carrots are tender.
6. Cook uncovered until the glaze has reduced, and the carrots are sticky and caramelized (approximately 5 minutes).
7. Serve with your favorite roast meat.

Tangy Veggie Coleslaw

Serves 8

1/2 small white cabbage, outer leaves removed
1/2 small red cabbage, outer leaves removed
4 large carrots, peeled
2 sticks of celery, trimmed and washed
1 daikon or 4 large radishes, peeled
1 red onion, peeled
2 cups mayonnaise
1 cup yogurt
1/4 cup Dijon or whole-grain mustard
Juice of 1 lemon
1/2 teaspoon sea salt
1 teaspoon freshly ground black pepper

1. Shred the vegetables using a mandoline or in a processor using the julienne blade.
2. In a medium bowl, whisk together the mayonnaise, yogurt, mustard, and lemon juice.
3. Pour the dressing over the vegetables, season with salt and pepper, and stir well to combine ingredients thoroughly.
4. Serve chilled.

Vegetable Tempura

Serves 8–10

1 cup each of firm vegetables and edible flowers (such as asparagus, broccoli, daylily, eggplant, leek, mushrooms, okra, red pepper, zucchini), cut into bite-size pieces

3 tablespoons soy sauce
1/4 cup rice vinegar
1 tablespoon honey
2 teaspoons finely grated ginger
1 cup all-purpose flour
1 tablespoon cornstarch
3/4 teaspoon fine sea salt
1 cup chilled seltzer water
Peanut or sunflower oil

1. Preheat oven to 300°F.
2. Make the dipping sauce: mix the soy sauce, vinegar, honey, and ginger together in a small bowl, and set aside.
3. In a large bowl sift together the flour, cornstarch, and salt, then whisk in the seltzer water.
4. Line a baking tray with parchment paper.
5. Fill a deep-fat frying pan or wok to one third with oil, and heat to 375°F.
6. Fry the vegetables in small batches; dip the first batch briefly into the batter, then carefully place in the hot oil.
7. Fry until crisp and golden, remove with a slotted spoon, and drain on the prepared trays. Keep each batch warm in the oven.
8. Allow the oil to come back to temperature before frying the remaining vegetables.
9. Serve immediately with the dipping sauce.

Warm Winter Salad

Serves 6

3 radicchio, quartered
3 slices country bread
1 tablespoon extra virgin olive oil
3 cloves garlic, peeled and finely sliced
1 large handful pine nuts
1 large handful raisins
3/4 cup balsamic vinegar
2 cups arugula leaves
1 1/2 cups feta cheese

1. Char the radicchio in a dry, very hot griddle pan until slightly blackened all over. Place in a large bowl.
2. Toast the slices of bread.
3. In a pan, heat the oil, add the garlic, pine nuts, and raisins, and gently fry until the garlic begins to turn golden.
4. Remove from the heat and immediately pour in the balsamic vinegar to finish the dressing. Leave to cool.
5. Tear the radicchio and bread into the bowl, pour in the dressing, and mix well.
6. Turn out onto a plate and top with the arugula leaves. Crumble the feta over the top. Serve immediately.

Mains

Bacon & Mushroom Flan

Serves 6

1 package of pie crust dough
1 tablespoon extra virgin olive oil
1 cup each sliced onions and mushrooms
6 large eggs, beaten
1 cup heavy cream
8 thick slices bacon, fried until just brown
1½ cups grated cheddar cheese
Salt and freshly ground black pepper

1. Preheat oven to 375°F.
2. Place pie crust into a deep-dish pie plate.
3. Heat the olive oil in a skillet over low heat, and cook the onions until tender.
4. Whisk together the eggs and cream.
5. Cut the bacon into small strips and place in the pie shell. Add the mushrooms, onions, and cheese.
7. Season the egg mixture, then pour into the pie shell and bake for 45 minutes or until the egg mixture is set.
6. Remove from the oven and allow to rest.
7. Serve warm or cold with fresh green salad and crusty bread, or new potatoes.

Garlic & Lemon Shrimp

Serves 4

4 teaspoons extra virgin olive oil
2 large red bell peppers, deseeded and diced
2 pounds asparagus, trimmed and cut into 1-inch lengths
Grated zest of half, and juice of whole lemon
½ teaspoon salt
2 cups snow peas
5 cloves garlic, minced
1 pound raw shrimp, peeled and cleaned
1 cup chicken stock, thickened with a teaspoon of cornstarch
2 tablespoons chopped fresh cilantro

1. Heat half the oil in a large wok or skillet over medium-high heat.
2. Add the peppers, asparagus, lemon zest, and salt; stir and cook for 3-4 minutes.
3. Add snow peas and cook for 1-2 minutes.
4. Transfer the vegetables to a warmed dish.
5. Heat the remaining oil, add the garlic and shrimp, and cook for 1 minute.
6. Add the stock, and cook, stirring, until the sauce has thickened slightly and the shrimp are pink and just cooked.
7. Remove from the heat. Stir in lemon juice and cilantro.
8. Pour the shrimp and sauce over the vegetables and serve with fragrant rice.

Mediterranean Kebabs

Serves 6

10 ounces halloumi cheese, cut into 1-inch cubes
1 yellow bell pepper, cored, deseeded, cut into 1-inch pieces
1 zucchini, cut into ¼-inch-thick half-moon slices
1 pint cherry tomatoes
Small bunch of mint, finely chopped
1 fresh red chili, deseeded and finely chopped
Finely grated zest of 1 lemon
2 tablespoons extra virgin olive oil
Freshly ground black pepper

1. Soak 6 wooden skewers in cold water to prevent them from burning.
2. Put all ingredients into a large bowl and stir well to thoroughly coat the cheese and vegetables with the marinade.
3. Thread the cheese and vegetables equally onto the skewers, and cook under the broiler on an oiled tray, turning once.
4. Serve with green salad and pitas or flatbreads.

Mustard-Baked Fish

Serves 4

4 (8-ounce) fish fillets
Salt and freshly ground black pepper
1 cup sour cream
3 tablespoons Dijon mustard
1 tablespoon whole-grain mustard
2 tablespoons minced shallots
2 teaspoons drained capers

1. Preheat the oven to 425°F.
2. Line a sheet pan with parchment paper. Place the fish fillets skin side down on the sheet pan. Sprinkle generously with salt and pepper.
3. Combine all other ingredients in a small bowl, season with salt and pepper, and stir well. Spread the sauce on the fish.
4. Bake for 10-15 minutes, until the fish flakes easily at the thickest part.
5. Serve straight from the pan with new potatoes and green beans or snap peas.

Noodles with Mushrooms and Spinach

Serves 4

1 tablespoon sesame or sunflower oil
4 small boneless, skinless chicken fillets, sliced thinly
4 ounces egg noodles
1 large bunch scallions, chopped
2 garlic cloves, chopped roughly
2½ cups sliced mushrooms
½ cup oyster sauce
1 cup chicken stock
1 cup chopped spinach
¼ cup toasted sesame seeds

1. Heat the oil in a skillet, add the chicken, season, and cook over high heat until browned, but not quite cooked through.
2. Meanwhile, cook the noodles as directed on the package, drain, and keep warm.
3. Stir the scallions, garlic, and mushrooms into the chicken, and cook for 2 minutes.
4. Add the oyster sauce, stock, and spinach, and cook for 2 minutes.
5. Serve sprinkled with seasame seeds on a bed of noodles.

Piquant Pasta

Serves 4

4–5 cups plum tomatoes, roughly chopped
Extra virgin olive oil
4 cloves garlic, minced
1 bunch basil, half of it sliced into strips
1 teaspoon chili flakes
Salt and freshly ground black pepper
¾ pound dried capellini or vermicelli
1 cup freshly grated Parmesan cheese
Extra grated Parmesan for serving

1. In a large bowl, mix together the plum tomatoes, olive oil, garlic, sliced basil, chili flakes, and 1 teaspoon each salt and pepper. Cover and set aside for a few hours.
2. Add 2 teaspoons of olive oil and 1 tablespoon of salt to a large pan of water, bring to a boil, and add the pasta.
3. Lower the heat and cook for 1–2 minutes until al dente. Drain and add to the bowl with the tomato mixture.
4. Add the cheese and toss well. Divide between individual pasta bowls, garnished with extra cheese and 2 basil leaves.

Potato & Squash Tagine

Serves 6

2 tablespoons extra virgin olive oil
2 medium onions, chopped
3 garlic cloves, minced
1 (15½-ounce) can tomatoes
2 tablespoons harissa
1 tablespoon each ground cinnamon and cumin
4 cups vegetable stock
2 large potatoes, peeled and roughly chopped
1 small winter squash, peeled, deseeded, and roughly chopped
1 cup chopped green beans
1 cup cherry tomatoes
2 tablespoons cornstarch mixed to a paste with water
Salt and freshly ground black pepper
Small bunch fresh cilantro

1. Heat the oil in a large skillet over low heat and fry the onion until soft.
2. Add the garlic, tomatoes, spices, and stock, bring to a boil, cover, and simmer for 10 minutes.
3. Add the potatoes, bring back to a boil, cover, and simmer for another 10 minutes.
4. Stir in the squash and green beans, and continue to cook, covered, for 5 minutes.
5. Add the tomatoes and simmer for 5 minutes more, then add the cornstarch paste to the stew and bring to a boil. Season to taste.
6. Garnish with cilantro leaves and serve with steamed couscous.

Satay Chicken & Peanut Dip

Serves 6–8

2 pounds skinless chicken breast fillets cut into 1-inch strips
¾ cup lemon juice
¾ cup extra virgin olive oil
2 shallots, minced
1½-inch piece fresh ginger root, minced
Salt and freshly ground black pepper
1 tablespoon fresh thyme leaves, chopped
1 tablespoon dark sesame oil
2 cloves garlic, minced
¼ teaspoon chili flakes, finely chopped
2 tablespoons white wine vinegar
¼ cup light brown sugar
2 tablespoons soy sauce
½ cup smooth peanut butter
2 tablespoons dry sherry
1½ teaspoons freshly squeezed lime juice

1. Place the chicken breasts in a glass bowl.
2. Whisk together the lemon juice, olive oil, half of the minced shallots and half of the ginger, salt, pepper, and thyme. Pour over

the chicken, cover, and marinate in the refrigerator for several hours.

3. Soak wooden-skewers in cold water to prevent them from burning.

4. Thread one chicken strip onto each skewer.

5. Heat the grill and cook the chicken breasts for 3–5 minutes on each side, until just cooked through.

6. For the peanut dip: In a small heavy-bottomed pan over medium heat, cook the sesame oil, garlic, the remainder of the shallots and ginger, and chili flakes for 10 minutes.

7. Whisk in the remaining ingredients and cook for 1 more minute. Cool.

8. Remove the chicken from the skewers and serve with fragrant white rice and individual bowls of peanut dip.

South Indian Curry

Serves 4

2 tablespoons sunflower oil
1 teaspoon mustard seeds
2 onions, peeled and finely sliced
2 fresh green chilies, deseeded and chopped
1 bunch curry leaves
1-inch piece ginger root, peeled and grated
1/2 teaspoon cumin seeds
1/2 teaspoon each ground chili powder, ground coriander, garam masala, and turmeric
6 tomatoes, chopped
2 sweet potatoes, peeled and cubed
1 large potato, peeled and cubed
Florets from 1 small cauliflower
1 eggplant, cubed
1/2 cup coconut milk
1 cup each string beans and peas
1 cup sliced okra
Salt and freshly ground black pepper

1. Heat the oil in a large pan, and fry the mustard seeds for 2–3 minutes. Stir in the onion, chilies, curry leaves, and ginger.

2. Add the cumin seeds and ground spices.

3. Cook, stirring all the time, over medium heat for 5 minutes.

4. Thoroughly stir in all of the vegetables.

5. Pour in the coconut milk and cook until the potato is soft and cooked through.

4. Add the beans, peas, and okra. Season and cook for a few more minutes until tender, and serve with basmati rice.

Spicy Bean Burgers

Serves 4

2 tablespoons sunflower oil
2 small onions, finely chopped
4 cloves garlic
2 red chili peppers, finely chopped
1 packed cup chopped spinach

2 (15 1/2-ounce) cans beans, such as cannellini or borlotti
1 cup fresh white breadcrumbs
1 tablespoon tomato paste
2 teaspoons each ground cumin and cinnamon
2 teaspoons chopped cilantro
Burger buns
Fresh, dressed mixed-leaf salad

1. Heat the oil in a pan and cook the onion, garlic, and chili peppers until soft, 4–5 minutes.

2. Cook the spinach for 2 minutes in hot, salted water, allow to cool, and squeeze out as much water from the spinach as possible.

3. Mash the beans well in a large bowl, then stir in the spinach, breadcrumbs, tomato paste, ground spices, and cilantro.

4. Add the onion mixture, season well, and stir thoroughly.

5. Wet your hands, divide the mixture into eight equal round portions.

6. Broil or fry as preferred for 3–4 minutes each side.

7. Place in burger buns or simply on the plate, and serve with salad leaves dressed with a salad dressing of your choice (see pages 281–282).

Stuffed Bell Peppers

Serves 4

4 large peppers, 2 red and 2 green
1/4 cup extra virgin olive oil
2 cups ground beef
1/2 cup onion, chopped small
1 (15 1/2-ounce) can tomatoes, chopped
1/4 cup fresh thyme, oregano, and basil
1/2 cup basmati rice, washed
1/2 cup water
1 teaspoon salt, plus extra for inside peppers
1 teaspoon Worcestershire sauce
1 cup sharp cheese, such as mature cheddar

1. Preheat oven to 350°F.

2. Slice the tops from the peppers; cut out the seeds and membranes, and sprinkle a little salt inside each pepper.

3. Heat the oil in a skillet. Cook ground beef and onion until browned and tender.

4. Add the tomatoes, herbs, rice, water, salt, and Worcestershire sauce.

5. Bring to a boil, reduce heat, cover, and simmer for 15 minutes.

6. Stir in the cheese, then stuff the peppers with the meat mixture.

7. Pack upright in an ovenproof dish, pour 1/4 cup water around the peppers, and bake, covered with aluminum foil, for 30 minutes.

8. Serve hot with crusty country bread.

Thai Spice Stir-Fry

Serves 4

2 tablespoons sunflower oil
2 shallots, peeled, halved, and sliced
1 cup each prepared vegetables: diced sweet
    potato, 3–4 inch lengths of asparagus,
    sliced runner beans, shredded bok choy
2 sticks lemongrass
3–4 Kaffir lime leaves
1 tablespoon Thai red curry paste
1½ cups vegetable stock
¾ cup coconut milk
Salt and freshly ground black pepper
½ cup peanuts, roughly chopped

1. Warm a wok or large pan over high
heat, add the oil, shallots, and sweet potato,
and stir-fry for 2 minutes.
2. Add the asparagus and runner beans
and stir-fry for 3 minutes, then stir in the
lemongrass, lime leaves, curry paste, and
stock, and simmer for 10 minutes.
3. Stir in the bok choy and coconut milk,
add seasoning, and heat thoroughly.
4. Serve with couscous and chopped
peanuts sprinkled over the vegetables.

Turkey Meatloaf

Serves 6–8

1½ pounds ground turkey
1 cup each finely chopped onion, sweet
    peppers, and celery
3 cloves garlic, minced
1 teaspoon each thyme and parsley
2 eggs, lightly beaten
½ cup ketchup
¾ cup fresh bread crumbs
2 teaspoons mustard powder
2 teaspoons Worcestershire sauce
Salt and freshly ground black pepper

1. Preheat oven to 350°F.
2. Thoroughly mix all ingredients together
in large mixing bowl. Lightly oil a 9 x
5-inch loaf pan, then pack in the mixture.
3. Cook in the oven for at least 1 hour; when
cooked, a meat thermometer inserted in the
middle should read 155°F.
4. Serve immediately with new potatoes
and a green vegetable. Alternatively, serve
cold with salad and fresh crusty bread.

Veggie Chili

Serves 6–8

2 tablespoons vegetable oil
2 large onions, chopped
4 large cloves garlic, minced
1 teaspoon each dried oregano, ground
    cinnamon, coriander, and paprika

3 tablespoons chili powder
1 (15½-ounce) can black beans or red
    kidney beans, drained and rinsed
¾ cup each dried green and red lentils
1 medium-size squash, peeled and diced
2 (14½-ounce) cans tomatoes
4 cups vegetable stock
1 each medium-size sweet green and red
    pepper, cored, deseeded, and diced
1 medium-size zucchini, diced
Salt and freshly ground pepper
Fresh cilantro to garnish

1. Heat the oil in large pan over medium
heat, add the onion, garlic, herbs, spices,
and chili powder, and cook for 5 minutes.
2. Stir in the beans, lentils, squash, and
tomatoes. Add the stock, cover, and cook for
30 minutes.
3. Add the remaining vegetables, cook for
another 30 minutes, and season to taste.
4. Garnish with cilantro; serve with plain
boiled rice, or jacket potatoes and sour cream.

Very Veggie Pie

Serves 6

¼ cup unsalted butter
2 medium-large onions, peeled and chopped
1½ cups sliced mushrooms
2 teaspoons each fresh oregano and thyme
¼ cup dry sherry
Salt and freshly ground black pepper
½ cup flour
2½ cups vegetable stock
¼ cup heavy cream
1½ cups each potatoes, carrots and
    parsnips, peeled and cut into ¾-inch dice
1½ cups broccoli florets
½ cup chopped parsley
1 packet of puff pastry or pie dough

1. Melt the butter in a large pot on medium
heat. Add the onions, fry until golden.
2. Add the mushrooms, oregano, and
thyme, stirring as they soften and brown.
3. Add the sherry, season with salt and
pepper, gradually stir in the flour, lower the
heat, and cook gently for 3–4 minutes.
4. Stir in the stock, bring to a boil, simmer
for 2 minutes, then stir in the cream.
5. In a pan of boiling, salted water, cook the
potatoes for 5 minutes, add the carrots and
parsnips, and cook for another 5 minutes.
6. Remove the vegetables from the pan, add
the broccoli, and blanch for 2 minutes.
7. Add the vegetables with the parsley to the
sauce, stir well, then pour into a pie dish.
8. Lay the pastry or pie dough over the top,
seal firmly around the edge of the dish, and
cut three slits in the crust for steam to escape.
9. Bake on a baking sheet at 375°F for
an hour, until the crust is golden.

Sauces & Pickles

Citrus & ginger Dressing

Serves 4–6

1½ tablespoons ginger syrup (see below)
3 tablespoons orange juice
1 tablespoon lime juice
3 tablespoons sugar
Salt and freshly ground black pepper

1. Whisk all ingredients together.
2. Use as part of a recipe or as a dressing.

Cranberry Sauce

Makes approx. 2 cups

12 ounces fresh cranberries, stoned, or
  1 (12-ounce) bag frozen cranberries
1 cup sugar
1 cup freshly squeezed orange juice
Grated zest of 1 orange*
1 teaspoon each grated nutmeg and
  ginger root*
2-inch cinnamon stick*

1. Combine all ingredients in a pan and
bring to a boil. Simmer until the berries
begin to break down.
2. When cool, transfer to a serving dish.

* VARIATION:
For a great accompaniment to the holiday
turkey, include the orange zest, nutmeg,
ginger, and cinnamon stick. Remove the
cinnamon stick before serving.

Ginger Syrup

Makes approx. 2 cups

1 cup roughly chopped ginger root
2 cups each sugar and water
1 tablespoon black peppercorns*

1. Put all ingredients in a medium pan,
and set over medium heat. Bring to a boil,
stirring until the sugar has dissolved.
2. Simmer for an hour, or until the liquid
has reduced by half.
3. Allow to cool, then strain through a fine
sieve or strainer.
4. Store in a jar in the refrigerator.
Use as dressing (see above), a sauce for
fruit desserts and ice creams, or mixed with
sparkling water for a cool summer drink.

* VARIATION:
Prepare ginger syrup recipe as above, but add
1 tablespoon of black peppercorns to the pan.

Herby Butter

Serves 4–6

¼ cup unsalted butter
3 tablespoons dry white wine
1 tablespoon chopped parsley
2 tablespoons chopped chives
2 teaspoons each chopped dill and sage
½ teaspoon salt

1. Melt the butter in a small pan over
medium-low heat.
2. Gradually stir in all other ingredients.
3. Use drizzled over fresh, steamed
vegetables.

Pesto

Makes 4 cups

½ cup pine nuts
5 cloves garlic, chopped
5 cups fresh basil leaves, packed tightly
Salt and freshly ground black pepper
1 cup extra virgin olive oil
1 cup freshly grated Parmesan cheese

1. Process the pine nuts and garlic in a
food processor for 30 seconds.
2. Add the basil leaves, 1 teaspoon of salt,
and some freshly ground pepper.
3. Slowly pour the olive oil into the bowl
and process until the mixture is
thoroughly puréed.
4. Add the Parmesan, purée until smooth.
5. Store the pesto in the refrigerator or
freezer with a thin film of olive oil on top if
not needed immediately.
6. Use as a sauce for pasta or with grilled
meat or fish.

Radish & Cilantro Dressing

Serves 4

1 cup radishes, finely chopped
1 teaspoon cumin seeds, toasted
1 small dried chili, finely chopped
Juice of 1 lime
2 tablespoons extra virgin olive oil
1 cup cilantro leaves, finely chopped

1. Place all ingredients into a small
bowl and mix thoroughly.
2. Use as an accompaniment for any
grilled meat or fish, or a curry dish.

Red Hot Salsa

Serves 4

4 fleshy tomatoes, deseeded and chopped
2 cloves garlic, minced
2 small red onions, finely chopped
1 small hot red chili, finely chopped
1 tablespoon each extra virgin olive oil;
   capers, chopped; fresh parsley, chopped
Salt and freshly ground black pepper

1. Combine all ingredients in a bowl, cover,
and refrigerate for several hours.
2. Use with tortilla and vegetable chips,
such as kale chips (see page 61), or as a
condiment.

Rich Cranberry & Shallot Gravy

Serves 4–6

1 bottle red wine
2 shallots, sliced
3 cloves garlic, minced
1 sprig rosemary
6 tablespoons cranberry sauce (see
   page 281)
1 tablespoon sugar
Salt and freshly ground black pepper

1. In a large pan bring the wine to a boil,
add the shallots, garlic, and rosemary, and
boil for 10 minutes to reduce.
2. Stir in the cranberry sauce and sugar,
and whisk vigorously.
3. Discard the rosemary, then season to taste.

Pickled Sunchokes

Makes 4 cups

1 medium onion, thinly sliced
1 cup each water and white vinegar
1/2 cup sugar
1/2 teaspoon each salt, mustard seeds,
   and mustard powder
1/4 teaspoon each celery seeds and chili
   flakes
2 pounds sunchokes

1. Put all ingredients except the sunchokes
in a large pan.
2. Peel and slice the sunchokes and add
immediately to the pan.
3. Over high heat, bring the mixture
to a boil.
4. Reduce the heat, simmer uncovered,
stirring occasionally, for 15 minutes.
5. Transfer the sunchokes and liquid
to a bowl, cover and refrigerate.
6. Serve with any cooked meats.

Sour cream, Chive & Mustard Sauce

Serves 4

1 cup sour cream
1 small bunch chives, trimmed and chopped
1 small onion, minced
1 tablespoon whole-grain mustard
1/4 teaspoon salt
Freshly ground black pepper
1 tablespoon chopped parsley

1. Put all ingredients into a small pan
and warm slowly over very low heat until
just hot.
2. Sprinkle over the chopped parsley and
serve immediately.
3. A good accompaniment for any
vegetable dish.

Tomato Vinaigrette

Serves 4

3 large ripe plum tomatoes, skinned,
   peeled, and roughly chopped
1 large garlic clove
1 small shallot, chopped
1/2 cup basil leaves
1 tablespoon sherry vinegar
Juice of half a lemon
1 tablespoon parsley leaves
Salt and freshly ground black pepper

1. Combine all ingredients in a blender
until smooth.
2. Use with any salad, but this is especially
good with feta and mozzarella salads.

Traditional French Vinaigrette

Makes 1 cup

1/2 teaspoon sea salt
1/4 cup red wine vinegar
2 small shallots, minced
1 clove garlic, minced
2 teaspoons Dijon mustard
1 cup extra virgin olive oil
Freshly ground black pepper

1. Mix together the salt, vinegar, shallots,
and garlic in a small bowl.
2. Stir in the mustard and olive oil, and
season with a little pepper.
3. Transfer to a serving jar and shake
well before using.
4. Ideal for any green or mixed-leaf salad.

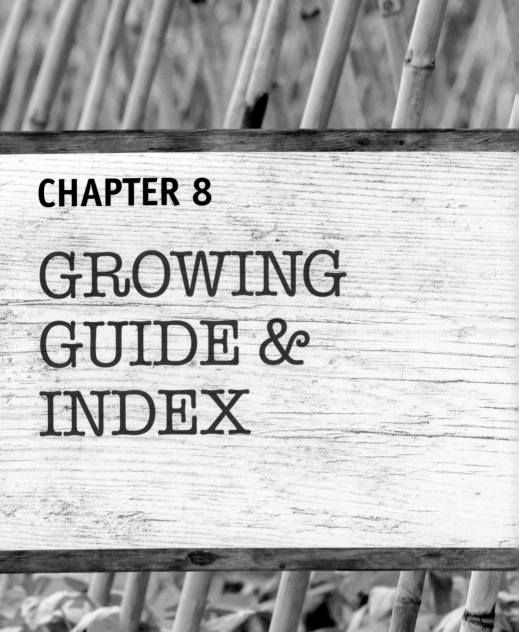

CHAPTER 8

GROWING GUIDE & INDEX

MAINTENANCE	ADZUKI BEAN	AMERICAN GROUNDNUT
AHS Heat Zone	----	----
USDA Hardiness Zone	10	3–7
Sun Exposure	Full sun	Shade to part sun
Height	12–24 inches	4–8 inches
Width	N/A	4–8 inches
Habit	Bushy	Trailing
Soil PH	Acidic, neutral	Acidic, alkaline, neutral
Soil Type	Loam, neutral	Loam, sand
Soil Drainage	Well drained	Low
Spacing	6 inches	N/A
Water Requirements	Average	Average
Suitable for Containers	Yes	Yes
Diseases	Bacterial stem rot, white mold, viruses	N/A
Pests	Lygus bugs, two-spotted spider mites	N/A

MAINTENANCE	ASPARAGUS	AVOCADO
AHS Heat Zone	8–1	12–10
USDA Hardiness Zone	3–8	10–11
Sun Exposure	Sun to part shade	Full sun
Height	12–48 inches	30–60 feet
Width	12–36 inches	20–80 feet
Habit	Bushy	Spreading
Soil PH	Alkaline, neutral	Acidic, alkaline, neutral
Soil Type	Clay, loam, sand	Clay, loam, sand
Soil Drainage	Well drained	Well drained
Spacing	10–25 inches	15–20 feet
Water Requirements	Average	Average
Suitable for Containers	No	No
Diseases	Anthracnose, asparagus rust, canker, crown and spear rot, fusarium wilt, leaf spot	Black spot, damping off, gray mold, fusarium wilt
Pests	Aphids, asparagus beetles, Japanese beetles, slugs, spider mites	Borers, caterpillars, lace bugs, mites, thrips

ARRACACHA	ARTICHOKE	ARUGULA
12–1	9–8	7–1
9–11	8–9	7–10
Full sun	Full to part sun	Full sun
6–60 inches	48–96 inches	12–24 inches
8–36 inches	36–48 inches	6–12 inches
Upright	Rosette	Clump-forming, rosette
Neutral	Acidic, alkaline, neutral	Acidic, neutral
Loam	Clay, loam	Loam
Well drained	Well drained	Well drained
————	48–72 inches	6 inches
Average water	Low	Average
No	Yes	Yes
Erwinia, leaf spot, sclerotinia, viruses	Botrytis, gray mold, powdery mildew, ramularia leaf spot, root rot	Bacterial leaf spot, downy mildew, white rust
Aphids, black cutworms, caterpillars, chisa beetles, nematodes, spider mites	Aphids, blackflies, lacewings, ladybug larvae, slugs, snails	Aphids, cabbage worms, flea beetles, nematodes, slugs, snails

BASIL	BEET GREENS	BEETROOT
11–1	12–1	12–1
9–11	6–10	6–10
Full sun	Full sun	Full sun
6–28 inches	12–24 inches	12–24 inches
6–24 inches	6–12 inches	6–12 inches
Clump-forming	Rosette	Rosette
Neutral	Alkaline, neutral	Alkaline, neutral
Loam, sand	Loam, sand	Loam, sand
Well drained	Well drained	Well drained
12–18 inches	3–4 inches	3–4 inches
Moderate	Average	Average
Yes	Yes	Yes
Black spot, damping off, gray mold, fusarium wilt	Cercospora leaf spot, root rot, scab	Cercospora leaf spot, root rot, scab
Aphids, Japanese beetles, slugs	Flea beetles, leafhoppers, leaf miners	Flea beetles, leafhoppers, leaf miners

MAINTENANCE	BELGIAN ENDIVE	BELL PEPPER
AHS Heat Zone	12–1	12–1
USDA Hardiness Zone	9–11	10–11
Sun Exposure	Full sun	Full sun
Height	7–8 inches	6–60 inches
Width	10–25 inches	8–36 inches
Habit	Upright	Clump-forming
Soil PH	Acidic, neutral	Acidic, alkaline, neutral
Soil Type	Loam	Clay, loam, sand
Soil Drainage	Well drained	Well drained
Spacing	8–9 inches	18–24 inches
Water Requirements	Average water	Average
Suitable for Containers	Yes	Yes
Diseases	Anthracnose, bacterial soft rot, septoria blight, bottom rot, damping off, downy mildew, fusarium wilt, mold	Bacterial spot, blossom-end rot, blight, canker, damping off, fusarium wilt, mosaic, powdery mildew, virus
Pests	Aphids, spider mites, caterpillars, darkling beetles, flea beetles, leaf miners, loopers, thrips	Aphids, cutworms, pepper armyworm, flea beetles, leaf miners, tomato fruit worms, pepper weevils, mites

MAINTENANCE	BITTER MELON	BROCCOLI
AHS Heat Zone	12–5	6–1
USDA Hardiness Zone	10–11	6–11
Sun Exposure	Full sun to part shade	Full to part sun
Height	8–15 feet	12–36 inches
Width	N/A	12–24 inches
Habit	Climbing	Upright
Soil PH	Acidic, alkaline, neutral	Neutral
Soil Type	Loam, sand	Loam, sand
Soil Drainage	Well drained	Well drained
Spacing	9–10 feet	12–24 inches
Water Requirements	Average	Average
Suitable for Containers	No	No
Diseases	Bacterial wilt, downy mildew, powdery mildew, viral diseases	Clubroot, downy mildew
Pests	Aphids, spider mites, spotted cucumber beetles, striped cucumber beetles	Aphids, cabbage loopers, cabbage worms, flea beetles, whiteflies

BLACK-EYED PEA	BLADDER CAMPION	BORAGE GREENS
12–7	12–1	3–3
5–11	5–9	5–10
Full to part sun	Full to part sun	Full sun to part shade
3–12 feet	12–24 inches	18–28 inches
6–12 inches	12–24 inches	12–24 inches
Climbing or upright	Clump-forming	Clump-forming
Acidic, alkaline, neutral	Acidic, neutral	Acidic, alkaline, neutral
Loam, sand	Loam, sand	Sandy loam to clay loam
Well drained	Well drained	Dry or moist
4 inches	9–12 inches	15 inches
Low	Low	Average
Yes	Yes	Yes
Bean mosaic virus	N/A	Powdery mildew
Aphids, bean beetles, caterpillars, grubs, leaf hoppers, mites, root-knot nematodes	N/A	Slugs, leaf-mining flies

BROCCOLINI	BROCCOLI RABE	BRUSSELS SPROUTS
6–1	6–1	6–1
6–11	6–11	7–11
Full to part sun	Full sun	Full to part sun
12–36 inches	12–18 inches	24–36 inches
12–24 inches	12 inches	12–24 inches
Upright	Upright	Upright
Neutral	Acidic to neutral	Neutral
Loam, sand	Loam, sand	Loam, sand
Well drained	Well drained	Well drained
12–24 inches	4–6 inches	14–24 inches
Average	Moderate	Average
No	Yes	No
Clubroot, downy mildew	Clubroot	Blackleg, black rot
Aphids, cabbage loopers, cabbage worms, flea beetles, whiteflies	Cabbage aphids, cabbage root maggots, cabbage worms, slugs, snails	Aphids, cabbage loopers, cabbage worms, caterpillars, flea beetles, leaf spots, thrips, slugs

MAINTENANCE	BURDOCK	CABBAGE
AHS Heat Zone	————	6–1
USDA Hardiness Zone	3–7	8–11
Sun Exposure	Part shade	Full to part sun
Height	3–6 feet	10–24 inches
Width	3 feet	12–30 inches
Habit	Clump-forming	Compact
Soil PH	Acidic, alkaline, neutral	Acid, neutral
Soil Type	Clay, loam, sand	Loam, sand
Soil Drainage	Well drained	Well drained
Spacing	6 inches	10–12 inches
Water Requirements	Average	Average
Suitable for Containers	Yes	No
Diseases	Powdery mildew	Blackleg, black rot, clubroot
Pests	Grasshoppers	Cabbage loopers, cabbage maggots, cabbage worms, cutworms

MAINTENANCE	CASSAVA	CAULIFLOWER
AHS Heat Zone	12–9	6–1
USDA Hardiness Zone	8–11	4–11
Sun Exposure	Full to part sun	Full sun
Height	7–12 feet	12–36 inches
Width	5–9 feet	12–24 inches
Habit	Upright	Clump-forming
Soil PH	Acidic, alkaline, neutral	Neutral
Soil Type	Loam, sand	Loam, sand
Soil Drainage	Average	Well drained
Spacing	24–36 inches	18–24 inches
Water Requirements	Low	Average
Suitable for Containers	No	No
Diseases	Anthracnose, bacterial blight, cassava mosaic disease, root rot	Botrytis, downy mildew, cabbage hernia
Pests	Cassava green mites, variegated grasshoppers	Cabbage maggots, cabbage moths, cabbage white butterflies

CAPERS	CARDOON	CARROT
12–4	9–1	10–1
8–11	7–10	3–9
Full sun	Full to part sun	Full sun
24–36 inches	36–72 inches	24–36 inches
Up to 60 inches	36–48 inches	12–24 inches
Shrubby	Upright	Clump-forming
Alkaline, neutral	Acidic, alkaline, neutral	Neutral
Sand	Clay, loam	Loam, sand
Well drained	Well drained	Well drained
36–48 inches	18–24 inches	3 inches
Low	Average	Average
Yes	No	Yes
Cercospora, powdery mildew, southern blight, white rust	Damping off, root rot	Black rot, cavity spot, damping off, leaf blight, sclerotinia rot, soft rot, downy/powdery mildew
Aphids, caterpillars, mealybugs, scale insects, whiteflies	Aphids, leafhoppers, leaf miners, slugs, snails	Aphids, carrot weevils, carrot rust flies, flea beetles, nematodes

CELERIAC	CELERY	CHICKPEA
9–3	8–10	----
8–9	2–10	----
Sun to part shade	Sun to light shade	Full to partial sun
12–36 inches	18–24 inches	8–40 inches
6–12 inches	12–18 inches	10–45 inches
Clump-forming	Upright	Mound-forming
Acidic, alkaline, neutral	Mildly acidic, neutral	Acidic, alkaline, neutral
Clay, loam, sand	Loam	Loam, sand
Well drained	Moist, well drained	Well drained
6–8 inches	12 inches	3–6 inches
Moderate	Heavy	Low
Yes	No	Yes
Celery leaf spot	Blight, carrot rust, pink rot	Anthracnose, blight, mosaic
Celery leaf miners, slugs	Aphids, celery worms, earwigs, nematodes, slugs	Aphids, flea beetles, leafhoppers, mites

MAINTENANCE	CHICORY	CHILI PEPPER
AHS Heat Zone	9–1	12–1
USDA Hardiness Zone	3–7	10–11
Sun Exposure	Full to part sun	Full sun
Height	24–48 inches	6–60 inches
Width	12–24 inches	8–36 inches
Habit	Clump-forming	Clump-forming
Soil PH	Acidic, alkaline, neutral	Acidic, alkaline, neutral
Soil Type	Clay, loam, sand	Clay, loam, sand
Soil Drainage	Well drained	Well drained
Spacing	8–9 inches	18–24 inches
Water Requirements	Average	Average
Suitable for Containers	Yes	Yes
Diseases	Anthracnose, bacterial soft rot, bottom rot, damping off, downy mildew, fusarium wilt, septoria blight, white mold	Mosaic virus, verticillium wilt
Pests	Aphids, darkling beetles, flea beetles, leaf miners, loopers, thrips, slugs, snails	Aphids, Colorado potato beetles, cutworms, pepper maggots, whiteflies

MAINTENANCE	COLLARD GREENS	CRESS
AHS Heat Zone	6–1	––––
USDA Hardiness Zone	7–11	6–9
Sun Exposure	Full to part sun	Full sun to part shade
Height	24–36 inches	4–6 inches
Width	18–24 inches	N/A
Habit	Rosette	Mat-forming
Soil PH	Acidic, neutral	Acidic, alkaline, neutral
Soil Type	Clay, loam, sand	Clay, loam, sand
Soil Drainage	Well drained	Moist
Spacing	12–18 inches	N/A
Water Requirements	Average	High
Suitable for Containers	Yes	Yes
Diseases	Black leg, black rot, clubroot	Alternaria leaf spot, anthracnose, black leg, black rot, damping off, downy mildew
Pests	Aphids, cabbage worms, flea beetles	Flea beetles

CHINESE ARTICHOKE	CHIVES	CHRYSANTHEMUM LEAVES
12–1	12–1	9–1
4–9	10–11	5–9
Full sun	Full sun	Full sun to part shade
12–18 inches	6–60 inches	18–24 inches
12–24 inches	8–36 inches	24–36 inches
Clump-forming	Clump-forming	Clump-forming
Neutral	Acidic, alkaline, neutral	Acidic, neutral
Clay, loam, sand	Clay, loam, sand	Loam
Well drained	Well drained	Well drained
9–12 inches	18–24 inches	12–15 inches
Average	Average	Average
Yes	Yes	Yes
Viral disease	Mosaic virus, verticillium wilt, bulb rot, fungal leaf spot, mildew, rust, smut	Botrytis, powdery mildew, rust, viruses
Aphids, beetle larvae, red spider mites, slugs, snails	Aphids, onion flies, thrips	Aphids, capsid bugs, earwigs, leaf miners, slugs, snails, thrips

CUCUMBER	DAIKON	DANDELION
12–1	––––	9–1
9–11	––––	3–9
Full to part sun	Full sun to part shade	Full sun to part shade
N/A	12–24 inches	6–12 inches
3–12 feet	6–12 inches	6–8 inches
Climbing	Rosette	Rosette
Neutral	Acidic, neutral	Neutral
Clay, loam, sand	Clay, loam, sand	Clay, loam, sand
Well drained	Well drained	Well drained
18–36 inches	4–6 inches	N/A
Moderate	Moderate	Low
No	No	N/A
Anthracnose, leaf spot, downy mildew, mosaic virus, powdery mildew, scab, stem blight	Clubroot	N/A
Aphids, cucumber beetles, red spider mites, whiteflies	Cabbage root maggots	N/A

MAINTENANCE	DAYLILY	DILL
AHS Heat Zone	9–2	12–1
USDA Hardiness Zone	4–9	0–11
Sun Exposure	Full to part sun	Full sun
Height	24–48 inches	12–36 inches
Width	18–32 inches	12–18 inches
Habit	Clump-forming	Upright
Soil PH	Acidic, alkaline, neutral	Acidic, alkaline, neutral
Soil Type	Clay, loam, sand	Loam
Soil Drainage	Average	Moist, well drained
Spacing	12–24 inches	12–18 inches
Water Requirements	Low	Average
Suitable for Containers	Yes	Yes
Diseases	Rust	Alternaria blight
Pests	Aphids, cabbage loopers, cabbage worms, flea beetles, whiteflies	Aster yellows, hornworms, parsley worms

MAINTENANCE	ENSETE	EGGPLANT
AHS Heat Zone	12–1	12–1
USDA Hardiness Zone	10–11	10–11
Sun Exposure	Full sun	Full sun
Height	12–30 feet	24–48 inches
Width	10–15 feet	12–24 inches
Habit	Upright	Clump-forming
Soil PH	Acidic, neutral	Neutral
Soil Type	Clay, loam	Clay, loam, sand
Soil Drainage	Well drained	Well drained
Spacing	N/A	18–24 inches
Water Requirements	Low	Average
Suitable for Containers	Ornamental varieties only	Yes
Diseases	Bacterial wilt	Verticillium wilt
Pests	N/A	Colorado potato beetles, cutworms, flea beetles, tomato hornworms

ELEPHANT FOOT YAM	ELEPHANT GARLIC	ENDIVE
————	————	10–1
10–11	5–10	8–1
Full sun	Full sun	Full to part sun
36–54 inches	18–24 inches	4–18 inches
24–36 inches	3–4 inches	6–24 inches
Upright	Upright	Clump-forming
Acidic	Neutral	Acidic, alkaline, neutral
Loam, sand	Clay, loam, sand	Clay, loam, sand
Well drained	Well drained	Well drained
24–36 inches	9–12 inches	12 inches
Average	Average	Moderate
No	Yes	Yes
Foot rot, leaf blight, mosaic	Botrytis, leaf blight, bulb and neck rot, downy mildew, purple blotch	Bottom rot, leaf spot, downy mildew, tip burn
Termites, white ants, mealybugs	Aphids, allium leaf mining flies, garlic bulb mites, leek moths, nematodes, thrips	Aphids, caterpillars, slugs, thrips

FAVA BEAN	FIDDLEHEAD	FISH MINT
10–6	9–1	12–1
8–11	4–9	5–11
Full sun	Full shade to part sun	Full shade to part sun
4–6 feet	4–6 feet	6–12 inches
N/A	3–5 feet	18–36 inches
Bushy	Upright	Mat-forming
Alkaline, neutral	Acidic, neutral	Acidic, neutral
Loam, sand	Loam	Clay, loam, sand
Well drained	Well drained, moist	Poorly drained to wet
5–6 inches	6–8 feet	8–12 inches
Average	Moderate	High
Yes	No	Yes
Anthracnose, blight, chocolate spot fungus, fava bean rust, mosaic	N/A	N/A
Aphids, bean beetles, flea beetles, leafhoppers, mites	Slugs	N/A

MAINTENANCE	FLORENCE FENNEL	FLUTED PUMPKIN
AHS Heat Zone	9–1	————
USDA Hardiness Zone	4–9	————
Sun Exposure	Full to part sun	Full sun
Height	24–48 inches	Up to 40 feet
Width	12–36 inches	Up to 40 feet
Habit	Upright	Climbing or trailing
Soil PH	Alkaline, neutral	Acidic
Soil Type	Clay, loam, sand	Loam, sand
Soil Drainage	Well drained	Well drained
Spacing	6–20 inches	5–6 feet
Water Requirements	Low	Average
Suitable for Containers	Yes	No
Diseases	Cercospora leaf blight, downy mildew, powdery mildew, rust	Angular leaf spot, anthracnose, cercospora leaf spot, downy mildew, pod rot
Pests	Aphids, armyworms, cutworms, root-knot nematodes	Cotton leaf rollers

MAINTENANCE	GREEN BEAN	GUAR
AHS Heat Zone	11–1	————
USDA Hardiness Zone	3–10	N/A
Sun Exposure	Full sun	Full sun
Height	Up to 13 feet	Up to 9 feet
Width	12–24 inches	36–40 inches
Habit	Climbing	Upright
Soil PH	Alkaline, neutral	Acidic, alkaline, neutral
Soil Type	Loam, sand	Loam, sand
Soil Drainage	Well drained	Well drained
Spacing	2–10 inches	N/A
Water Requirements	Average	N/A
Suitable for Containers	Bush varieties only	No
Diseases	Bacterial blight, bean common mosaic virus, white mold	Alternaria leaf spot, bacterial blight
Pests	Aphids, leafhoppers, Mexican bean beetles, seedcorn maggots, spider mites	Gall midges, guar midges

GARLIC	GARLIC CHIVES	GINGER
9–1	12–1	12–9
4–9	4–8	8–15
Full sun	Full sun	Sun to part shade
18–24 inches	12 inches	24–48 inches
6–8 inches	12 inches	36–72 inches
Upright	Clump-forming	Clump-forming
Acidic, alkaline, neutral	Acidic, alkaline, neutral	Acidic, neutral
Loam, sand	Clay, loam, sand	Loam, sand
Well drained	Well drained	Well drained
4–6 inches	8 inches	15 inches
Average	Low	Average
Yes	Yes	Yes
Downy mildew, garlic mosaic virus, purple blotch, rust, white rot	Bulb rot, fungal leaf spot, mildew, rust, smut	Bacterial soft rot, bacterial wilt, rhizome spots
Bulb mites, leaf miners, nematodes, onion maggots, thrips	Aphids, onion flies, thrips	Chinese rose beetles, root-knot nematodes

HORSERADISH	INDIAN PEA	IVY GOURD
12–1	8–1	––––
3–10	9–10	8–11
Full sun to part shade	Full sun	Full sun to light shade
2–5 feet	24–36 inches	8–10 feet
24 inches	24–36 inches	N/A
Clump-forming	Trailing or climbing	Climbing
Acidic, neutral	Acidic, alkaline, neutral	Acidic, alkaline, neutral
Clay, loam	Clay, loam, sand	Clay, loam, sand
Well drained	Well drained	Well drained
20–30 inches	6–10 inches	3–8 feet
Moderate	Low	Average
Yes	Yes	No
Bacterial leaf spot, brittle root, cercospora leaf spot, mosaic, ramularia leaf spot, white rust	Downy mildew, powdery mildew, fusarium wilt, rust	Anthracnose, black rot, powdery mildew, mosaic, stem rot
Cabbage worms, flea beetles	Aphids, thrips	Aphids, clearwing moths, coreid bugs, fruit flies, pumpkin caterpillars, weevils

MAINTENANCE	KALE	KOHLRABI
AHS Heat Zone	6–1	6–1
USDA Hardiness Zone	7–11	7–11
Sun Exposure	Full sun to part shade	Full to part sun
Height	18–36 inches	12–36 inches
Width	12–36 inches	12–18 inches
Habit	Rosette	Rosette
Soil PH	Neutral to part alkaline	Neutral
Soil Type	Loam	Loam, sand
Soil Drainage	Moist	Well drained
Spacing	15 inches	6 inches
Water Requirements	Average	Moderate
Suitable for Containers	Yes	Yes
Diseases	Black rot, downy mildew	Alternaria, black leg, bacterial rot, cabbage yellows, downy mildew
Pests	Aphids, cutworms, flea beetles	Aphids, cabbage loopers, cabbage worms, cutworms, flea beetles, nematodes, slugs, snails

MAINTENANCE	LEMONGRASS	LENTIL
AHS Heat Zone	9–1	––––
USDA Hardiness Zone	10–11	––––
Sun Exposure	Full to part sun	Full sun
Height	3–6 feet	18 inches
Width	36 inches	6–8 inches
Habit	Clump-forming	Upright
Soil PH	Acidic, neutral	Acidic, alkaline, neutral
Soil Type	Loam, sand	Clay, loam, sand
Soil Drainage	Average	Well drained
Spacing	36 inches	18–24 inches
Water Requirements	Moderate	Average
Suitable for Containers	No	Yes
Diseases	Leaf blight, little leaf	Ascochyta blight, fusarium root rot, rhizoctonia, sclerotinia
Pests	Spider mites	Aphids, lygus bugs, seedcorn maggots, thrips, wireworms

KURRAT	LAMB'S LETTUCE	LEEK
————	12–1	7–1
5–9	5–11	5–9
Full sun	Full to part sun	Full sun to part shade
18–24 inches	3–12 inches	12–36 inches
6–12 inches	4–12 inches	12–24 inches
Upright	Rosette	Upright
Neutral	Acidic, neutral	Acidic, alkaline, neutral
Clay, loam, sand	Loam, sand	Clay, loam, sand
Well drained	Well drained	Well drained
9–12 inches	3–6 inches	4–6 inches
Average	Average	Moderate
Yes	Yes	Yes
Sclerotium fungus, purple blotch, rust, white tip	Powdery mildew, rust, fungus	Botrytis, leaf blight, purple blotch, rust
Nematodes, thrips	Aphids, caterpillars, flea beetles, leaf miners, slugs, snails, thrips	Onion maggots, slugs, thrips

LETTUCE	LIMA BEAN	LOTUS ROOT
12–1	————	12–3
————	6–11	10–11
Full sun to part shade	Full sun	Full to part sun
6–24 inches	10–12 feet	12–48 inches
6–24 inches	N/A	3–8 feet
Clump-forming, upright	Climbing, trailing	Clump-forming
Neutral	Acidic, alkaline, neutral	Neutral
Loam	Clay, loam, sand	Clay, loam
Well drained	Well drained	Wet soil
12 inches	6–10 inches	N/A
Average	Average	High
Yes	Bush varieties only	Yes
Damping off, downy mildew, lettuce rot, mosaic, fusarium	Anthracnose, blight, mosaic	Fusarium wilt
Aphids, cabbage loopers, cutworms, leafhoppers, leaf miners, slugs, wireworms	Bean leaf rollers, bean weevils, flea beetles, leafhoppers, mites	Aphids, caddisworms, leaf rollers, spider mites, whiteflies

MAINTENANCE	LUPINI	MASHUA
AHS Heat Zone	1–9	————
USDA Hardiness Zone	8–11	7–10
Sun Exposure	Full sun to part shade	Full sun
Height	Up to 48 inches	7–13 feet
Width	12 inches	3–6 feet
Habit	Clump-forming	Climbing, trailing
Soil PH	Acidic, neutral	Acidic, neutral
Soil Type	Clay, loam, sand	Loam, sand
Soil Drainage	Well drained	Well drained
Spacing	18–24 inches	30 inches
Water Requirements	Average to low	Average
Suitable for Containers	Yes	Yes
Diseases	Powdery mildew	Mosaic virus
Pests	Aphids	N/A

MAINTENANCE	MUSTARD	NAPA CABBAGE
AHS Heat Zone	————	9–3
USDA Hardiness Zone	5–9	6–11
Sun Exposure	Sun to part shade	Full to part sun
Height	12–16 inches	6–36 inches
Width	12 inches	6–24 inches
Habit	Clump-forming	Upright
Soil PH	Acidic, alkaline, neutral	Acidic, neutral
Soil Type	Clay, loam, sand	Clay, loam, sand
Soil Drainage	Well drained	Well drained
Spacing	N/A	12–18 inches
Water Requirements	Average	Average
Suitable for Containers	No	Yes
Diseases	Alternaria, black spot, clubroot, damping off, sclerotinia stem rot, turnip mosaic virus, white rust	Alternaria leaf spot, anthracnose, blackleg, damping off, downy mildew, clubroot, powdery mildew
Pests	Armyworms, flea beetles, cabbage seedpod weevils, cutworms, diamond back moths, grasshoppers	Aphids, armyworms, flea beetles, cabbage worms, cutworms, moth larvae, cabbage loopers, thrips

MOTH BEAN	MUNG BEAN	MUSHROOM
12	----	N/A
----	----	N/A
Full sun	Full sun	None
12–18 inches	24–30 inches	N/A
N/A	N/A	N/A
Creeping, mat-forming	Upright	N/A
Acidic, alkaline, neutral	Acidic, neutral	N/A
Clay, loam, sand	Loam, sand	N/A
Well drained	Well drained	N/A
6–9 inches	2–4 inches	N/A
Low	Average	Well drained
No	Yes	Yes
Root and seedling blight, yellow mosaic virus	Root and stem rot, blight, gummy pod, powdery mildew, legume little leaf, puffy pod, tan spot, virus	Bacterial blotch, cobweb, dry/wet bubble, trichoderma
Nematodes	Aphids, bean pod borers, bean flies, caterpillars, *Helicoverpa*, mirids, pod-sucking bugs, thrips	Cecid, phorid, and sciarid flies; mites; nematodes

NOPAL	OKRA	OLIVE
----	12–4	10–8
8–11	5–11	8–10
Full sun	Full sun	Full sun
15–20 feet	4–6 feet	15–40 feet
Up to 16 feet	2 feet	12–25 feet
Spreading	Upright	Rounded
Acidic, alkaline, neutral	Acidic, alkaline, neutral	Alkaline, neutral
Loam, sand	Clay, loam, sand	Loam, sand
Well drained	Well drained	Well drained
4–6 feet	18–24 inches	5–20 feet
Low	Low	Low
Yes	Yes	No
Anthracnose, charcoal, fungus, phyllosticta pad spots, root rot, scab	Leaf spot, cercospora blight, damping off, fusarium wilt, powdery mildew, verticillium wilt	Galls, olive anthracnose, olive berry rot, olive shield, olive warts, peacock spot, sooty mold, verticillium wilt
Blind June beetles, cactus eating moths, cochineals, chinch bugs, borers, thrips, wireworms, zebra worms	Corn earworms, cabbage loopers, flea beetles, fruit and stem borers, jassids, root-knot nematodes	Olive fruit flies

MAINTENANCE	ONION	PAK CHOY (BOK CHOY)
AHS Heat Zone	12–1	9–3
USDA Hardiness Zone	10	6–11
Sun Exposure	Full to part sun	Full to part sun
Height	2–3 feet	6–36 inches
Width	4–12 inches	6–24 inches
Habit	Upright	Upright
Soil PH	Neutral	Acidic, neutral
Soil Type	Loam, sand	Loam, sand
Soil Drainage	Well drained	Clay, loam, sand
Spacing	4–6 inches	6–12 inches
Water Requirements	Average	Average
Suitable for Containers	Yes	Yes
Diseases	Downy mildew, neck rot, rust, shanking, white rot, white tip disease	Alternaria leaf spot, anthracnose, damping off, downy mildew, clubroot, powdery mildew
Pests	Leek moths, onion flies, onion leaf miners, onion eelworms, root maggots	Beet armyworms, cutworms, cabbage aphids, loopers, cabbage worms, diamondback moths, flea beetles, thrips

MAINTENANCE	PEAS	PEANUT
AHS Heat Zone	12–1	9
USDA Hardiness Zone	3–11	8–11
Sun Exposure	Full to part shade	Full to part sun
Height	1–8 feet	10–12 inches
Width	N/A	12–36 inches
Habit	Climbing	Upright or bushy
Soil PH	Neutral	Acidic, neutral
Soil Type	Clay, loam, sand	Loam, sand
Soil Drainage	Well drained	Well drained
Spacing	6–8 inches	24–36 inches
Water Requirements	Average	Average
Suitable for Containers	No	Yes
Diseases	Fusarium wilt, powdery mildew, mosaic virus, root rot	Black rot, blight, leaf spot, peanut bud necrosis, rust, stem rot, stunt, wilt virus
Pests	Aphids, pea weevils, slugs, thrips	Root-knot nematode, thrips, two-spotted spider mites

PARSLEY	PARSLEY ROOT	PARSNIP
9–1	9–1	7–1
6–9	5–9	4–9
Full to part sun	Full sun to part shade	Full sun
12–36 inches	12–13 inches	6–60 inches
12–24 inches	12–24 inches	3–6 inches
Clump-forming	Clump-forming	Rosette
Neutral	Neutral	Neutral
Loam, sand	Loam, sand	Loam
Well drained	Well drained	Well drained
10–12 inches	10–12 inches	3–4 inches
Average	Average	Average
Yes	Yes	No
Septoria leaf spot, stem rot	Parsnip canker	Black rot, damping off, downy/powdery mildew, parsnip canker, root rot, watery soft rot, viruses
Carrot weevils, flea beetles, leafhoppers, tarnished plant bugs	Carrot weevils, flea beetles, leafhoppers, tarnished plant bugs	Aphids, beet armyworms, carrot rust flies, cutworms, leaf miners, swallowtail and moth larvae

PEARL ONION	PEA SHOOTS	PIGEON PEA
7–1	12–1	――――
5–9	3–11	9–11
Full sun to part shade	Full sun to some shade	Full to part sun
12 inches	6 inches	8–40 inches
2–4 inches	N/A	10–45 inches
Upright	Mat-forming	Mound-forming
Acidic, neutral	Acidic, alkaline, neutral	Acidic, alkaline, neutral
Loam	Clay, loam, sand	Loam, sand
Well drained	Well drained	Well drained
2 inches	N/A	3–6 inches
Average	Average	Low
Yes	Yes	Yes
Botrytis, leaf blight, purple blotch, rust	Powdery mildew, damping off, root rot	Anthracnose, blight, mosaic
Onion maggots, slugs, thrips	Aphids, cutworms, pea and bean weevils	Aphids, flea beetles, leafhoppers, mites

MAINTENANCE	PIGNUT	POTATO
AHS Heat Zone	————	12–13
USDA Hardiness Zone	————	6–11
Sun Exposure	Full sun to part shade	Full to part sun
Height	12–18 inches	18–24 inches
Width	6–12 inches	16–30 inches
Habit	Clump-forming	Clump-forming
Soil PH	Acidic, neutral	Neutral
Soil Type	Clay, loam, sand	Loam
Soil Drainage	N/A	Well drained
Spacing	N/A	12–15 inches
Water Requirements	N/A	Average
Suitable for Containers	N/A	Yes
Diseases	N/A	Fungal blight, potato blackleg, potato rot, potato scab
Pests	N/A	Carrot flies, potato beetles, snails, slugs

MAINTENANCE	PURSLANE	RADICCHIO
AHS Heat Zone	12–1	9–1
USDA Hardiness Zone	8–11	4–10
Sun Exposure	Full to part sun	Full to part sun
Height	2–10 inches	6 inches
Width	12–24 inches	4 inches
Habit	Mat-forming, trailing	Dense rosette
Soil PH	Acidic, alkaline, neutral	Acidic, alkaline, neutral
Soil Type	Loam, sand	Loam, sand
Soil Drainage	Well drained	Well drained
Spacing	N/A	8–12 inches
Water Requirements	Low	Moderate
Suitable for Containers	Yes	Yes
Diseases	Crown rot	Powdery mildew, tomato spotted wilt, white mold
Pests	Aphids	Root maggots, wireworms, thrips

PRAIRIE TURNIP	PRUSSIAN ASPARAGUS	PUMPKIN
————	————	12–1
4–8	5–9	9–11
Full sun	Full sun to shade	Full sun
12 inches	24 inches	12–36 inches
12 inches	8 inches	5–15 feet
Clump-forming	Upright	Trailing
Acidic, alkaline, neutral	Alkaline, neutral	Acidic, neutral
Clay, loam, sand	Clay, loam, sand	Loam
Well drained	Well drained	Well drained
N/A	12 inches	18–36 inches
Average	Low	Average
N/A	Yes	No
N/A	N/A	Bacterial wilt, downy mildew, powdery mildew, scab, viral diseases
N/A	N/A	Aphids, spider mites, squash bugs, striped cucumber beetles

RADISH	RAMPS	RUNNER BEAN
8–11	————	1–11
5–11	4–7	9–11
Full sun	Part sun to shade	Full sun to part shade
4–10 inches	4–18 inches	10–20 feet
4–6 inches	6–12 inches	24 inches
Rosette	Clump-forming	Climbing, trailing
Acidic, neutral	Alkaline, neutral	Alkaline, neutral
Loam, sand	Loam	Clay, loam, sand
Well drained	Average	Well drained
1 inch	N/A	6–9 inches
Average	Moderate	Moderate
Yes	No	Yes
Alternaria blight, black root, clubroot, damping off, downy mildew, fusarium wilt, scab, white rust	Septoria leaf spot	Anthracnose, halo blight, fusarium wilt, runner bean and French bean rust
Cabbage root maggots, flea beetles, swede midges	N/A	Red spider mites, southern green stinkbugs

MAINTENANCE	RUTABAGA	SALSIFY
AHS Heat Zone	9–3	10–1
USDA Hardiness Zone	2–11	4–10
Sun Exposure	Full sun	Full to part shade
Height	12–24 inches	16–60 inches
Width	12 inches	8–12 inches
Habit	Rosette	Clump-forming
Soil PH	Acidic, neutral	Acidic, neutral
Soil Type	Loam, sand	Loam, sand
Soil Drainage	Well drained	Well drained
Spacing	6 inches	4 inches
Water Requirements	Average	Average
Suitable for Containers	No	No
Diseases	Alternaria, anthraconose, clubroot, powdery mildew	N/A
Pests	Aphids, cutworms, flea beetles, loopers, root maggots, wireworms	Carrot rust flies, wireworms

MAINTENANCE	SORREL	SOYBEAN
AHS Heat Zone	6–1	2–11
USDA Hardiness Zone	3–7	7–10
Sun Exposure	Full to part sun	Full sun
Height	24–40 inches	2–6 feet
Width	12–24 inches	2–3 feet
Habit	Clump-forming	Upright
Soil PH	Acidic, neutral	Acidic, alkaline, neutral
Soil Type	Loam	Loam, sand
Soil Drainage	Average	Well drained
Spacing	12–18 inches	4–6 inches
Water Requirements	Low	Moderate
Suitable for Containers	Yes	Yes
Diseases	N/A	Anthracnose, blight, brown spot, downy and powdery mildew, root and stem rot, soybean rust, viruses
Pests	Aphids	Alfalfa hoppers, beet armyworms, beetles, caterpillars, corn earworms, cloverworms, stinkbugs

SHALLOT	SNAP PEA	SNOW PEA
12–1	12–1	12–1
2–11	3–11	3–11
Full to part sun	Full to part sun	————
12–36 inches	36–48 inches	12–48 inches
4–12 inches	12 inches	12 inches
Clump-forming	Climbing	Climbing
Neutral	Acidic, neutral	Neutral
Loam, sand	Clay, loam, sand	Clay, loam, sand
Well drained	Well drained	Well drained
3–5 inches	3–6 inches	1–2 inches
Average	Average	Average
Yes	Yes	Yes
Anthracnose, botrytis, blight, blotch, downy mildew, onion white rot, pink root, smut	Downy mildew, fusarium wilt, powdery mildew, root rot	Downy mildew, fusarium wilt, powdery mildew, root rot
Lesser bulb flies, onion flies, onion maggots, thrips	Aphids, cutworms, mites, pea weevils, seedcorn maggots, thrips	Aphids, cutworms, mites, pea weevils, seedcorn maggots, thrips

SPINACH	SUMMER SQUASH	SUMMER SQUASH BLOSSOMS
2–11	12–1	12–1
6–9	9–11	9–11
Full sun to part shade	Full sun	Full sun
18–24 inches	24–36 inches	24–36 inches
12–24 inches	24–36 inches	24–36 inches
Rosette	Climbing	Climbing
Alkaline, neutral	Neutral	Neutral
Loam, sand	Loam, sand	Loam, sand
Well drained	Well drained	Well drained
18–24 inches	18–30 inches	18–30 inches
Average	Moderate	Moderate
Yes	Yes	Yes
Anthracnose, blight, cercospora leaf spot, cucumber mosaic disease, downy mildew, rust	Bacterial wilt, downy mildew, powdery mildew, scab, viral diseases	Bacterial wilt, downy mildew, powdery mildew, scab, viral diseases
Aphids, spinach leaf miners, slugs	Cucumber beetles, slugs, snails, squash bugs, vine borers	Cucumber beetles, slugs, snails, squash bugs, vine borers

MAINTENANCE	SUNCHOKE	SWEET POTATO
AHS Heat Zone	9–1	12–1
USDA Hardiness Zone	3–9	11–12
Sun Exposure	Full to part sun	Full sun
Height	5–10 feet	2–20 feet
Width	24–48 inches	Up to 5 feet
Habit	Upright	Climbing
Soil PH	Acidic, alkaline, neutral	Acidic, alkaline, neutral
Soil Type	Clay, loam, sand	Clay, loam, sand
Soil Drainage	Average	Well drained
Spacing	24 inches	12–18 inches
Water Requirements	Low	Average
Suitable for Containers	Yes	Yes
Diseases	Fungal diseases, tobacco mosaic virus	Alternaria blight, bacterial soft rot, bacterial wilt, black rot, fusarium root and stem rot, pox, leaf and stem scab
Pests	Nematodes	Cucumber beetles, flea beetles, sweet potato weevils, whitefringed beetles, grubs, wireworms

MAINTENANCE	TINDA	TOMATO
AHS Heat Zone	N/A	12–1
USDA Hardiness Zone	N/A	8–11
Sun Exposure	Full sun	Full sun
Height	48 inches	1–20 feet
Width	N/A	1–4 feet
Habit	Trailing	Clump-forming
Soil PH	Acidic, neutral	Acidic
Soil Type	Loam, sand	Loam, sand
Soil Drainage	Well drained	Well drained
Spacing	20–24 inches	12–36 inches
Water Requirements	Average	Average
Suitable for Containers	Yes	Yes
Diseases	Fruit rot, downy mildew, powdery mildew	Blossom-end rot, catface, early blight, fusarium wilt, late blight, verticillium wilt
Pests	Aphids, leaf beetles, melon fruit flies, thrips, white flies	Aphids, Colorado potato beetles, cutworms, flea beetles, tomato hornworms

SWISS CHARD	TARO	TEPARY BEAN
12–1	12–7	7–10
6–10	8–15	————
Full sun	Full to part sun	Full sun
12–24 inches	36–72 inches	Up to 10 feet
12–24 inches	36–60 inches	36–48 inches
Clump-forming	Clump-forming	Climbing, trailing
Alkaline, neutral	Acidic, neutral	Acidic, alkaline, neutral
Loam, sand	Clay, loam, sand	Sand, loam
Well drained	Low	Well drained
12–18 inches	15–24 inches	6 inches
Average	Moderate	Low
Yes	Yes	Bush varieties only
Cercospora leaf spot	CBDV virus, leaf blight, leaf spot, root and corm rot, mosaic virus	Beet curly top virus, halo blight, mosaic virus, white mold disease
Aphids, mites, caterpillars	Aphids, pink hibiscus mealybugs, red spider mites, taro beetles	Potato leafhoppers, Mexican bean beetles

TOMATILLO	TIGERNUT	TURMERIC
12–1	12–1	12–1
N/A	5–11	8–11
Full sun	Full to part sun	Full sun to part shade
24–48 inches	12–24 inches	24–36 inches
36–48 inches	N/A	12 inches
Semi-upright	Mat-forming	Clump-forming
Neutral	Acidic, alkaline, neutral	Acidic, alkaline, neutral
Clay, loam, sand	Clay, loam, sand	Loam, sand
Well drained	Average	Well drained
12–18 inches	N/A	18–24 inches
Average	Low	Moderate
Yes	Yes	Yes
Blight, fungal leaf spot, powdery mildew, viruses	N/A	Leaf spot, rhizome rot
Cutworms, European corn borers, flea beetles, fruit worms, leaf miners, mites, tomato hornworms	N/A	Aphids, nematodes, shoot borers, spider mites

MAINTENANCE	TURNIP	TURNIP GREENS
AHS Heat Zone	9–3	9–3
USDA Hardiness Zone	6–11	6–11
Sun Exposure	Full to part sun	Full to part sun
Height	12–24 inches	12–24 inches
Width	18 inches	8–18 inches
Habit	Rosette	Rosette
Soil PH	Acidic, neutral	Acidic, neutral
Soil Type	Clay, loam, sand	Clay, loam, sand
Soil Drainage	Well drained	Well drained
Spacing	4–6 inches	4–6 inches
Water Requirements	Average	Average
Suitable for Containers	Yes	Yes
Diseases	Anthracnose, black/white leaf spot, clubroot, damping off, downy mildew, blight, turnip mosaic	Anthracnose, black/white leaf spot, clubroot, damping off, downy mildew, blight, turnip mosaic
Pests	Aphids, cabbage worms, cutworms, flea beetles, root maggots, wireworms	Aphids, cabbage worms, cutworms, flea beetles, root maggots, wireworms

MAINTENANCE	WATERCRESS	WELSH ONION
AHS Heat Zone	8–1	9–1
USDA Hardiness Zone	3–9	6–9
Sun Exposure	Full to part sun	Full to part sun
Height	6–18 inches	18–24 inches
Width	12–36 inches	3–4 inches
Habit	Mat-forming	Upright
Soil PH	Neutral	Neutral
Soil Type	Loam, sand	Loam, sand
Soil Drainage	Wet	Well drained
Spacing	3–4 inches	6 inches
Water Requirements	High	Average
Suitable for Containers	Yes	Yes
Diseases	Crook root, turnip mosaic virus	Downy mildew, purple blotch, Welsh onion yellow stripe virus, white rot
Pests	Snails, spider mites, white flies	American bollworms, beet armyworms, onion thrips

VANILLA	WASABI	WATER CHESTNUT
12–10	4–1	12–1
10–15	7–10	8–11
Full sun to part shade	Full to part shade	Full sun
Up to 100 feet	12 inches	18–36 inches
––––	8 inches	36 inches
Climbing	Clump-forming	Upright
Neutral	Acidic, neutral	Alkaline, neutral
Loam	Clay, loam, sand	Clay, loam
Well drained	Low	Low
6–7 feet	12 inches	30 inches
Average	High	High
Yes	Yes	Yes
Anthracnose, black rot, fusarium, rust, stem blight	Black leg, clubroot, damping off, downy mildew, black rot, white mold, white rust, vascular wilt	Rot, fungus
Ash gray weevils, caterpillars, earwigs, lamellicorn beetles, slugs, snails	Aphids, crane flies, moths, slugs	Water birds

WEST INDIAN GHERKIN	WHEATGRASS	WINGED BEAN
12–1	10–1	––––
9–11	2–24	9–11
Full to part sun	Full sun	Full sun
3–12 feet	N/A	9–12 feet
3–12 feet	N/A	N/A
Climbing	Mat-forming	Climbing
Neutral	Neutral	Acidic, alkaline, neutral
Clay, loam, sand	Loam	Clay, loam, sand
Well drained	Average	Average
18–36 inches	N/A	6 inches
Moderate	Average	Moderate
No	Yes	Yes
Anthracnose, leaf spot, downy mildew, mosaic virus, powdery mildew, scab, stem blight	Leaf and stem rust, smut	Powdery mildew
Aphids, cucumber beetles, red spider mites, whiteflies	Ergots, grasshoppers	Nematodes, mites

MAINTENANCE	WINTER MELON	WINTER SQUASH
AHS Heat Zone	————	————
USDA Hardiness Zone	9–11	9–11
Sun Exposure	Full sun	Full sun
Height	N/A	N/A
Width	N/A	N/A
Habit	Climbing	Climbing
Soil PH	Acidic, neutral	Acidic, neutral
Soil Type	Loam, sand	Loam, sand
Soil Drainage	Well drained	Well drained
Spacing	12 inches	12 inches
Water Requirements	Moderate	Moderate
Suitable for Containers	Dwarf variety only	Dwarf variety only
Diseases	Bacterial wilt, blossom-end rot, downy mildew, fusarium wilt, powdery mildew	Bacterial wilt, blossom-end rot, downy mildew, fusarium wilt, powdery mildew
Pests	Aphids, cucumber beetles, cutworms, mites, pickleworms, squash bugs, squash mine borers	Aphids, cucumber beetles, cutworms, mites, pickleworms, squash bugs, squash mine borers

MAINTENANCE	YAM	YARDLONG BEAN
AHS Heat Zone	10–7	————
USDA Hardiness Zone	9–10	————
Sun Exposure	Full to part sun	Full to part sun
Height	30–40 feet	6–12 feet
Width	36–48 inches	N/A
Habit	Climbing	Climbing
Soil PH	Neutral	Acidic, alkaline, neutral
Soil Type	Loam, sand	Loam, sand
Soil Drainage	Well drained	Well drained
Spacing	20 inches	8 inches
Water Requirements	Low	Average
Suitable for Containers	No	No
Diseases	Anthracnose	————
Pests	Mealybugs	Aphids, mites, thrips

YACÓN

12–6
7–11
Full to part sun
5–7 feet
24–36 inches
Upright
Acidic, alkaline, neutral
Clay, loam, sand
Well drained
24–36 inches
Average
No
Aster yellows, cucumber mosaic virus, wilt
Caterpillars, slugs

YARROW

9–1
3–9
Full sun
12–36 inches
12–36 inches
Clump-forming
Acidic, alkaline, neutral
Clay, loam, sand
Well drained
12–24 inches
Dry to medium
Yes
Botrytis, mold, powdery mildew, root rot
Aphids, mealybugs, thrips

INDEX

Garlic flowers

Vegetable harvest

ACKNOWLEDGMENTS

1 Wollertz/Shutterstock.com • 2–3 Ev Thomas/Shutterstock.com • 7 Roman Prishenko/Shutterstock.com • 8tl Chamille White/Shutterstock.com • 8tr Cgissemann/Shutterstock.com • 8b Jiang Hongyan/Shutterstock.com • 9tl Valentyn Volkov/Shutterstock.com • 9tr istetiana/Shutterstock.com • 9b Maya Kruchankova/Shutterstock.com • 10bl Michael Westhoff/istockphoto.com • 10c B Brown/Shutterstock.com • 10crb, br Keith Homan/Shutterstock.com • 11l B Brown/Shutterstock.com • 11c Philippe Rousselot/Shutterstock.com • 11r Tim Streater • 12tl Graham Taylor Photography/Shutterstock.com • 12tr joyfuldesigns/Shutterstock.com • 12cr homydesign/Shutterstock.com • 12cl Shutterstock.com • 12bl Chris Martin • 12br, 13tl Jani Bryson/istockphoto.com • 13tr Wayne Thume • 13cl Dvortygirl • 13cl Sergio Bertino/Shutterstock.com • 13cr Vladnik/Shutterstock.com • 13b Lee Valley & Veritas • 14–15b Ttstudio/Shutterstock.com • 15t Olivier Le Queinec/Shutterstock.com • 16–17 Johnny Adolphson/Shutterstock.com • 18t Ksenia Ragozina/Shutterstock.com • 18bl Philip Bird LRPS CPAGB/Shutterstock.com • 18br kuvona/Shutterstock.com • 19t Tolikoff Photography/Shutterstock.com • 19bl Shabbychef • 19br martiapunts/Shutterstock.com • 20t Ingrid Balabanova/Shutterstock.com • 20br Henrik Larsson/Shutterstock.com • 20bl Bochkarev Photography/Shutterstock.com • 21t pamuk/Shutterstock.com • 21bl Voyagerix/Shutterstock.com • 21br selbst gemach • 22tl magicinfoto/Shutterstock.com • 22cl fedsax/Shutterstock.com • 22cr Dream79/Shutterstock.com • 22bl thatreec/Shutterstock.com • 22br NoRegret/Shutterstock.com • 23t Magdalena Zurawska/Shutterstock.com • 23b Voyagerix/Shutterstock.com • 24t GoodMood Photo/Shutterstock.com • 24bl natalia bulatova/Shutterstock.com • 24bc Dionisvera/Shutterstock.com • 24br zstock/Shutterstock.com • 25tr Andrea J Smith/Shutterstock.com • 25bl Robert Biedermann/Shutterstock.com • 25br Roger Meerts/Shutterstock.com • 26t Vadym Zaitsev/Shutterstock.com • 26bl Victor M. Vicente Selvas • 26br Sherjaca/Shutterstock.com • 27 Maria Meester/Shutterstock.com • 28t J. Marijs/Shutterstock.com • 28cl dreamnikon/Shutterstock.com • 28bl Marbury/Shutterstock.com • 28br Emma manners/Shutterstock.com • 29cl Humannet/Shutterstock.com • 29cr picturepartners/Shutterstock.com • 29b lorenzo_graph/Shutterstock.com • 30tr Rowena Dumlao-Giardina/Shutterstock.com • 30tl Brent Hofacker/Shutterstock.com • 30bl Michele Paccione/Shutterstock.com • 30br littleny/Shutterstock.com • 31 Brent Hofacker/Shutterstock.com • 32bl Winning7799/Shutterstock.com • 33tr, c Elena Rostunova/Shutterstock.com • 33b Cgissemann/Shutterstock.com • 34t JBDesign/Shutterstock.com • 34bl Gordon Bell/Shutterstock.com • 34br Karl Allgaeuer/Shutterstock.com • 35t Panyajampatong/Shutterstock.com • 35background Voyagerix/Shutterstock.com • 36t Laitr Keiows/Shutterstock.com • 36cl JamesChen/Shutterstock.com • 36cr Wjarek/Shutterstock.com • 36b Winning7799/Shutterstock.com • 37t Apiguide/Shutterstock.com • 37bl Dourleak/Shutterstock.com • 37br Elena Rostunova/Shutterstock.com • 38t Susan Law Cain/Shutterstock.com • 38bl Slavapolo/Shutterstock.com • 38br Clematis • 39tl Ermess/Shutterstock.com • 39tr Sfocato/Shutterstock.com • 39b Gts/Shutterstock.com • 40tl nop16/Shutterstock.com • 40–41b Gordon Bell/Shutterstock.com • 41t Dream79/Shutterstock.com • 41cr Alex Sun/Shutterstock.com • 42t Darkone • 42cl Toni Genes/Shutterstock.com • 42bl Africa Studio/Shutterstock.com • 42br Urbanbuzz/Shutterstock.com • 43t Bablo/Shutterstock.com • 43b Andrew Koturanov/Shutterstock.com • 44t ChildofMidnight • 44c Rosesmith/Shutterstock.com • 45 Bakusova/Shutterstock.com • 46t Chantel/Shutterstock.com • 46b Barry Blackburn/Shutterstock.com • 47tr Bonchan/Shutterstock.com • 47cl Brent Hofacker/Shutterstock.com • 47cr Mona Makela/Shutterstock.com • 48t locrifa/Shutterstock.com • 48cl Tolikoff Photography/Shutterstock.com • 48br Monkey Business Images/Shutterstock.com • 49t Andrew Buckin/Shutterstock.com • 49br Barna Tanko/Shutterstock.com • 50t Mmcool/Shutterstock.com • 50c Jiang Hongyan/Shutterstock.com • 50cl Roberto Zilli/Shutterstock.com • 50crb Alexander Mazurkevich/Shutterstock.com • 50bl Roobcio/Shutterstock.com • 50bc Oleg Vinnichenko/Shutterstock.com • 50br Spasta/Shutterstock.com • 51 Richie Chan/Shutterstock.com • 52cr Weblogiq/Shutterstock.com • 52br Alzbeta/Shutterstock.com • 53tr Ldprod/Shutterstock.com • 53ca Aneta_Gu/Shutterstock.com • 53cb Dmitry Kalinovsky/Shutterstock.com • 53b fotoknips/Shutterstock.com • 54t Ruud Morijn Photographer/Shutterstock.com • 54cb enzodebernardo/Shutterstock.com • 54br Rossa di sera/Shutterstock.com • 54bl elena moiseeva/Shutterstock.com • 55 Buquet Christophe/Shutterstock.com • 56t Roman Pyshchyk/Shutterstock.com • 56b Andrew Buckin/Shutterstock.com • 57c Erika J Mitchell/Shutterstock.com • 57bl Roobcio/Shutterstock.com • 57br Stefan Holm/Shutterstock.com • 58cl Wouter Hagens • 58cr T.W. van Urk/Shutterstock.com • 58br Cardioceras • 59t, c TopTropicals.com • 59b R. R. Schippers • 60t Praphan Jampala/Shutterstock.com • 60c Katarzyna Mazurowska/Shutterstock.com • 60b Ruud Morijn Photographer/Shutterstock.com • 61t My Lit'l Eye/Shutterstock.com • 61bl c12/Shutterstock.com • 61br Vicuschka/Shutterstock.com • 62tl Fotyma/Shutterstock.com • 62cl 1000 Words/Shutterstock.com • 62b nomegrown.blogspot.co.uk • 63tl Voyagerix/Shutterstock.com • 63br Dream79/Shutterstock.com • 64t apiguide/Shutterstock.com • 64bl Monkey Business Images/Shutterstock.com • 64br Jamie Rogers/Shutterstock.com • 65t Geshas/Shutterstock.com • 65cr Miguel Garcia SaavedraI/Shutterstock.com • 65bl chinahbzyg/Shutterstock.com •

65br paintings/Shutterstock.com • 66t Tramont_ana/Shutterstock.com • 66bl Captain Yeo/Shutterstock.com • 66br Kelvin Wong/Shutterstock.com • 67t Bernhard Richter/Shutterstock.com • 67bl Alex Staroseltsev/Shutterstock.com • 67cr Bernhard Richter/Shutterstock.com • 67br rick seeney/Shutterstock.com • 78tl Seleznov Oleksandr/Shutterstock.com • 68c jeep2499/Shutterstock.com • 68b Quanthem/Shutterstock.com • 68br urbanbuzz/Shutterstock.com • 69 Can Balcioglu/Shutterstock.com • 70t Anna Hoychuk/Shutterstock.com • 70b Amarita/Shutterstock.com • 71tr isak55/Shutterstock.com • 71cr margouillat photo/Shutterstock.com • 71bl sangkhom sangkakam/Shutterstock.com • 71br natalia bulatova/Shutterstock.com • 72t Kati Molin/Shutterstock.com • 72bl yuris/Shutterstock.com • 72br Roobcio/Shutterstock.com • 72br pjhpix/Shutterstock.com • 73tr ChaiyonS021/Shutterstock.com • 73cl 6th Happiness • 73bl voranat/Shutterstock.com • 73bc Naowarat Jangprai/Shutterstock.com • 73br sutipong/Shutterstock.com • 74t Sally Wallis/Shutterstock.com • 74cr LogicheCreative.it/Shutterstock.com • 74br Natalija Sahraj/Shutterstock.com • 75tl Simone Andress/Shutterstock.com • 75cr EQRoy/Shutterstock.com • 75br hsagencia/Shutterstock.com • 76bl Denis and Yulia Pogostins/Shutterstock.com • 76bl Iryna_Kolesova/Shutterstock.com • 76br Rasbak • 77tl Margoe Edwards/Shutterstock.com • 77b Voyagerix/Shutterstock.com • 77br Tomás Fano • 78tr yuris/Shutterstock.com • 78c muratart/Shutterstock.com • 78b tusharkoley/Shutterstock.com • 79tl Heike Rau/Shutterstock.com • 79br aspen rock/Shutterstock.com • 79bl Joshua Resnick/Shutterstock.com • 80tl ocophoto/Shutterstock.com • 80b Andi Berger/Shutterstock.com • 81tl Jeff Wasserman/Shutterstock.com • 81tr KN/Shutterstock.com • 81b siraphat/Shutterstock.com • 82t GSPhotography/Shutterstock.com • 82bl peuceta/Shutterstock.com • 82br Natalia Mylova/Shutterstock.com • 83t optimarc/Shutterstock.com • 83cr Pedarilhos/Shutterstock.com • 83cb Scott Sanders/Shutterstock.com • 83br Roobcio/Shutterstock.com • 84t iravgustin/Shutterstock.com • 84c Gregory A. Pozhvanov/Shutterstock.com • 84bl Boumen Japet/Shutterstock.com • 84br Olena Kaminetska/Shutterstock.com • 85t Mark Herreid/Shutterstock.com • 85c JBDesign/Shutterstock.com • 85b Hgalina/Shutterstock.com • 86–87 Mirko Sobotta/Shutterstock.com • 88 joloei/Shutterstock.com • 89t MSPhotographic/Shutterstock.com • 89b TFoxFoto/Shutterstock.com • 90tc I love photo/Shutterstock.com • 90tr Mediagram/Shutterstock.com • 90cl Andrei Nekrassov/Shutterstock.com • 90br Bratwustle/Shutterstock.com • 91tr Roobcio/Shutterstock.com • 91crb Chris Bradshaw/Shutterstock.com • 91cb Dallas Events Inc/Shutterstock.com • 91clb David Reilly/Shutterstock.com • 91bl picturepartners/Shutterstock.com • 91bc Natalia Mylova/Shutterstock.com • 91br luckyraccoon/Shutterstock.com • 92t Sutichak Yachiangkham/Shutterstock.com • 92cl Denis and Yulia Pogostins/Shutterstock.com • 92br Teri Virbickis/Shutterstock.com • 92bl duckeesue/Shutterstock.com • 93t R.Iegosyn/Shutterstock.com • 93b Kevin M. Kerfoot/Shutterstock.com • 94l foto76/Shutterstock.com • 94r Praiwun Thungsarn/Shutterstock.com • 95t An Nguyen/Shutterstock.com • 95br H. Zell • 96t Vlad Siaber/Shutterstock.com • 96b jeff gynane/Shutterstock.com • 97t StockLite/Shutterstock.com • 97tl Voyagerix/Shutterstock.com • 97b Eugenio Hansen, OFS • 98t Denis and Yulia Pogostins/Shutterstock.com • 98b David Kay/Shutterstock.com • 99tl Robyn Mackenzie/Shutterstock.com • 99tr Norikazu/Shutterstock.com • 99b Miansari66 • 100 Thanat/Shutterstock.com • 101t prajit48/Shutterstock.com • 101cr sta/Shutterstock.com • 101br GreenTree/Shutterstock.com • 102t Natali Glado/Shutterstock.com • 102bl kitty45/Shutterstock.com • 102br An Nguyen/Shutterstock.com • 103t Natali Glado/Shutterstock.com • 103cr nuwatphoto/Shutterstock.com • 103bl Cbenjasuwan/Shutterstock.com • 103br foto76/Shutterstock.com • 104t risteski goce/Shutterstock.com • 104b evronphoto/Shutterstock.com • 105t irina d'elena/Shutterstock.com • 105c JIL Photo/Shutterstock.com • 105b blackboard1965/Shutterstock.com • 105bl Voyagerix/Shutterstock.com • 106t Smileus/Shutterstock.com • 106b divinecusine/Shutterstock.com • 107t Brent Hofacker/Shutterstock.com • 107b Dobryanska Olga/Shutterstock.com • 108t kostrez/Shutterstock.com • 108b yuris/Shutterstock.com • 109b Tomaszrp • 110t Fotokostic/Shutterstock.com • 110br Catherine Murray/Shutterstock.com • 111b Voyagerix/Shutterstock.com • 111br dcwcreations/Shutterstock.com • 112t An Nguyen/Shutterstock.com • 112bl Zigzag Mountain Art/Shutterstock.com • 112br Angel DiBilio/Shutterstock.com • 113t Harry Huber/Shutterstock.com • 113b Brent Hofacker/Shutterstock.com • 114tr Orange Line Media/Shutterstock.com • 114tl Shulevskyy Volodymyr/Shutterstock.com • 114cl David Kay/Shutterstock.com • 114bl bjonesphotography/Shutterstock.com • 114br Zigzag Mountain Art/Shutterstock.com • 115t Shebeko/Shutterstock.com • 115br Zigzag Mountain Art/Shutterstock.com • 116tl USGS Native Bee Inventory and Monitoring Program • 116b kschrei/Shutterstock.com • 117tl Izf/Shutterstock.com • 117tr bjul/Shutterstock.com • 118l nayneung1/Shutterstock.com • 118r huyangshu/Shutterstock.com • 119r bonchan/Shutterstock.com • 120–121 phloen/Shutterstock.com • 122t Gardendreamer/Dreamstime.com • 122b leungchopan/Shutterstock.com • 123t Midori • 123b Reika/Shutterstock.com • 124t Helena Jacoba • 124bl Adam Peterson • 124br Wendell Smith • 125t Malte • 125bl Roobcio/Shutterstock.com • 125br Tim Mainiero/Shutterstock.com • 126t Earth100 • 126b Crepesoles/Shutterstock.com • 127t ZEF/Shutterstock.com • 127b Colloidial/Shutterstock.com

ACKNOWLEDGMENTS

• 128t, bl Sever180/Shutterstock.com • 128br O.Bellini/Shutterstock.com • 129tr margouillat photo/Shutterstock.com • 129br picturepartners/Shutterstock.com • 130t Yangghao/Shutterstock.com • 130bc Steve Allen/Shutterstock.com • 130bl Marie C Fields/Shutterstock.com • 131t Honeyhuyue • 131b giovanni1/Shutterstock.com • 132t juniart/Shutterstock.com • 132b smereka/Shutterstock.com • 133cl Larry Korb/Shutterstock.com • 133tr Alexandra Lande/Shutterstock.com • 133bl, br Valentyn Volkov/Shutterstock.com • 133bc Diana Taliun/Shutterstock.com • 134t Enviu • 134c Ton Rulkens • 134br M. Unal Ozmen/Shutterstock.com • 134bl Quintinz • 135t, bl H. Zell • 135br Swapan Photography/Shutterstock.com • 136t Lorraine Swanson/Shutterstock.com • 136b sarayuth3390/Shutterstock.com • 136crb Tamasflex • 136br Tamara Kulikova/Shutterstock.com • 137cl Kuttelvaserova Stuchelova/Shutterstock.com • 137 Shebeko/Shutterstock.com • 138t c-monster • 138b nature10/Shutterstock.com • 139tl Henk Jacobs/Shutterstock.com • 139tr Olga_Phoenix/Shutterstock.com • 139br Lilyana Vynogradova/Shutterstock.com • 139bl Roobcio/Shutterstock.com • 140tl zhannaprokopeva/Shutterstock.com • 140cl basel101658/Shutterstock.com • 140br Debu55y/Shutterstock.com • 141tl Pefkos/Shutterstock.com • 141tr SusaZoom/Shutterstock.com • 141br Silvy78/Shutterstock.com • 142bl Simone van den Berg/Shutterstock.com • 143t Dinesh Valke • 143c Ekaterina Garyuk/Shutterstock.com • 143b Voyagerix/Shutterstock.com • 143br wasanajai/Shutterstock.com • 144tl anat chant/Shutterstock.com • 144b Leyla Ismet/Shutterstock.com • 145t Igor Dutina/Shutterstock.com • 145bl jreika/Shutterstock.com • 145br Luigi Guarino • 146cl Ruud Morijn Photographer/Shutterstock.com • 146bl Elenamiv/Shutterstock.com • 146br Shaiith/Shutterstock.com • 147t Magdanatka/Shutterstock.com • 147cr An Nguyen/Shutterstock.com • 148t Thanamat Somwan/Shutterstock.com • 148b Amawasri Pakdara/Shutterstock.com • 149b Diana Taliun/Shutterstock.com • 149t icollector.com • 150 Peter Etchells/Shutterstock.com • 151t yuqun/Shutterstock.com • 151bl Frankie Coburn • 151br trueepicure • 152t Kolidzei/Shutterstock.com • 152cl Olga_Phoenix/Shutterstock.com • 152cr MRS.Siwaporn/Shutterstock.com • 152bl Evlakhov Valeriy/Shutterstock.com • 152br Ozgur Coskun/Shutterstock.com • 153t Daimond Shutter/Shutterstock.com • 153br StevanZZ/Shutterstock.com • 153bl Igor Normann/Shutterstock.com • 154t NatalieJean/Shutterstock.com • 154bl joyfuldesigns/Shutterstock.com • 154br zi3000/Shutterstock.com • 155t Alexey Stiop/Shutterstock.com • 155cr, bl zkruger/Shutterstock.com • 155br Robyn Mackenzie/Shutterstock.com • 156t jlbuyz/Shutterstock.com • 156clb, bl successo images/Shutterstock.com • 156br KPG_Payless/Shutterstock.com • 157 sima/Shutterstock.com • 158t joloei/Shutterstock.com • 158bl sunsetman/Shutterstock.com • 158br wasanajai/Shutterstock.com • 159tl MRS.Siwaporn/Shutterstock.com • 159tr nookieme/Shutterstock.com • 159bl supersaiyan3/Shutterstock.com • 159br Wagaung • 160–161 pittawut/Shutterstock.com • 162t Valentyn Volkov/Shutterstock.com • 162b Guna Leite/Shutterstock.com • 163t background Voyagerix/Shutterstock.com • 163t Wallraf-Richartz Museum, Germany • 163b Garrytowns at English Wikipedia • 164l Alastair Wallace/Shutterstock.com • 164r Xufanc • 165 sanddebeautheil/Shutterstock.com • 166t HildaWeges Photography/Shutterstock.com • 166br mama_mia/Shutterstock.com • 166bl Sharon Day/Shutterstock.com • 167t Africa Studio/Shutterstock.com • 167c Singkham/Shutterstock.com • 167b Voyagerix/Shutterstock.com • 168t gorillaimages/Shutterstock.com • 168br Drozdowski/Shutterstock.com • 168bl Zaira Zarotti/Shutterstock.com • 169t Lilyana Vynogradova/Shutterstock.com • 169b Heike Brauer/Shutterstock.com • 170t Daderot • 170b Vezzani Photography/Shutterstock.com • 171t Javier Martin • 171b Iakov Filimonov/Shutterstock.com • 172t Forest & Kim Starr • 172bl sigur/Shutterstock.com • 172br Zigroup-Creations/Shutterstock.com • 173t Otmar Smit/Shutterstock.com • 173b Ekaterina Nikitina/Shutterstock.com • 174t Ussr79/Shutterstock.com • 174b Pixeljoy/Shutterstock.com • 175t JIL Photo/Shutterstock.com • 175c Bibliothèque nationale de France • 175bl ffolas/Shutterstock.com • 175br HG Photography/Shutterstock.com • 176t joloei/Shutterstock.com • 176b WingkLEE • 177t Rasica/Shutterstock.com • 177b liza1979/Shutterstock.com • 178t Altin Osmanaj/Shutterstock.com • 178bl merc67/Shutterstock.com • 178br J. S. Fisher/Shutterstock.com • 179t Jasenlee • 179b Claudio Divizia/Shutterstock.com • 180t konmesa/Shutterstock.com • 180b satit_srihin/Shutterstock.com • 181t showcake/Shutterstock.com • 181b Visun Khankasem/Shutterstock.com • 182t T. Voekler • 182b Maggiezhu/Shutterstock.com • 183t Mawardi Bahar/Shutterstock.com • 183b wasanajai/Shutterstock.com • 184t MRS.Siwaporn/Shutterstock.com • 184cl Jiang Hongyan/Shutterstock.com • 184c Peripitus • 184b Veronick/Shutterstock.com • 185t earnearn/Shutterstock.com • 185bl Mai-Linh Đoàn • 185br KENPEI • 186bl Claude Renault • 186br Pro_bug_catcher • 186t Franz Xaver • 187t nndrln/Shutterstock.com • 187b Thelmadatter • 188t Tagstock1/Shutterstock.com • 188b Elena Shashkina/Shutterstock.com • 189c Karen Sarraga/Shutterstock.com • 189b Dream79/Shutterstock.com • 190bl BrindleT • 190br Songpan Janthong/Shutterstock.com • 190t Dezidor • 191t GiryaGirl • 191cl Ask27 • 191cr Jeremy Keith • 191br Radka1/Shutterstock.com • 191bl Hans Braxmeier • 192t Hardyplants at English Wikipedia • 192b Fritzflohrreynolds • 193t Nadiatalent • 193b MrBill3 • 194t LianeM/Shutterstock.com • 194c Manuel Ploetz/Shutterstock.com • 194b witoon214/Shutterstock.com • 195t Dolce • 195b Radomil • 196t Piotr Debowski/Shutterstock.com • 196b Carlos Amarillo/Shutterstock.com • 197t Quayside/Shutterstock.com • 197br Barry Blackburn/Shutterstock.com • 197bl Roobcio/Shutterstock.com • 198t Jean-Pol Grandmont • 198b frankenstoen • 199t Kuttelvaserova Stuchelova/Shutterstock.com • 199cl Leif K-Brooks • 199cr Kajano/Shutterstock.com • 199bl Gertjan Hooijer/Shutterstock.com • 200–201 An Nguyen/Shutterstock.com • 202t Tatiana Volgutova/Shutterstock.com • 202b VicushkaI/Shutterstock.com • 203t Yulia Davidovich/Shutterstock.com • 203b verca/Shutterstock.com • 204t Nadezhda Nesterova/Shutterstock.com • 204b doniks/Shutterstock.com • 205t Anton Watman/Shutterstock.com • 205c Kei Shooting/Shutterstock.com • 205b AS Food studio/Shutterstock.com • 206t Nadezhda Nesterova/Shutterstock.com • 206b Wollertz/Shutterstock.com • 207t KellyNelson/Shutterstock.com • 207b James Clarke/Shutterstock.com • 208t Michaelpuche/Shutterstock.com • 208b Yeko Photo Studio/Shutterstock.com • 209tl Natalia Korshunova/Shutterstock.com • 209tr Jeff Wasserman/Shutterstock.com • 209cr blanche/Shutterstock.com • 209br chanwangrong/Shutterstock.com • 210t NorGal/Shutterstock.com • 210b An Nguyen/Shutterstock.com • 211t encikcasper/Shutterstock.com • 211b Sura Nualpradid/Shutterstock.com • 212t Dancing Fish/Shutterstock.com • 212c Mariemily Photos/Shutterstock.com • 212b Geo-grafika/Shutterstock.com • 213t sanddebeautheil/Shutterstock.com • 213bl Foodpictures/Shutterstock.com • 213br Contrail/Shutterstock.com • 214t Humannet/Shutterstock.com • 214c Kentaro Foto/Shutterstock.com • 214b KVdV/Shutterstock.com • 215t phadungsak sawasdee/Shutterstock.com • 215c Swapan Photography/Shutterstock.com • 215b Amawasri Pakdara/Shutterstock.com • 216t, bl Abdurrahman (Kenelm Piers Alexander) McCausland Permaculture Design Consultant and Trainer • 216br H. Zell • 217 J. Brew • 218t baitong333/Shutterstock.com • 218br grafvision/Shutterstock.com • 218bl Golden House/Shutterstock.com • 219l Jojoo64/Shutterstock.com • 219r mama_mia/Shutterstock.com • 220t Zinaida Zaiko/Shutterstock.com • 220b Lissandra Melo/Shutterstock.com • 221tl unpict/Shutterstock.com • 221tr HandmadePictures/Shutterstock.com • 221br Malivan_Iuliia/Shutterstock.com • 222t Michael Hermann • 222c Dr. Morley Read/Shutterstock.com • 222b In Tune/Shutterstock.com • 223 Michael Hermann • 224tl Nils Z/Shutterstock.com • 224b papkin/Shutterstock.com • 224tr nicobatista/Shutterstock.com • 225 Malivan_Iuliia/Shutterstock.com • 226t Iryna Loginova/Shutterstock.com • 226b sarsmis/Shutterstock.com • 227t CWA Studios/Shutterstock.com • 227c Barbro Bergfeldt/Shutterstock.com • 227b Rosser • 228t Madlen/Shutterstock.com • 228b ER_09/Shutterstock.com • 229t Elzbieta Sekowska/Shutterstock.com • 229b Brent Hofacker/Shutterstock.com • 230tl Charlotte Lake/Shutterstock.com • 230tr Ttatty/Shutterstock.com • 230b joyfuldesigns/Shutterstock.com • 231t Marina Onokhina/Shutterstock.com • 231cl Stanjoman/Shutterstock.com • 231br Sarah Jessup/Shutterstock.com • 231bl Bildagentur Zoonar GmbH/Shutterstock.com • 232t Matt Lavin • 232br John Pozniak • 233bl Allison • 233t Kingarion/Shutterstock.com • 233c anucha maneechote/Shutterstock.com • 233crb phloen/Shutterstock.com • 233br Varts/Shutterstock.com • 234t Iakov Filimonov/Shutterstock.com • 234c Bildagentur Zoonar GmbH/Shutterstock.com • 234b Paul_Brighton/Shutterstock.com • 235t hjochen/Shutterstock.com • 235bl Mirages.nl/Shutterstock.com • 35br Bildagentur Zoonar GmbH/Shutterstock.com • 236t Matt Ragen/Shutterstock.com • 236b wasanajai/Shutterstock.com • 237t vladf/Shutterstock.com • 237b Lilyana Vynogradova/Shutterstock.com • 238 Mr Suwit Gaewsee-Ngam/Shutterstock.com • 239t An Nguyen/Shutterstock.com • 239c Peerawat Aupala/Shutterstock.com • 239b Sony Ho/Shutterstock.com • 240t J. Aa./Shutterstock.com • 240b Eric Broder Van Dyke/Shutterstock.com • 241 vanillaechoes/Shutterstock.com • 242t Jerry Oldenettel • 242b Hamiza Bakirci/Shutterstock.com • 243 Fernando Sanchez Cortes/Shutterstock.com • 244t Sanit Fuangnakhon/Shutterstock.com • 244b Suwan Wanawattanawong/Shutterstock.com • 245t KPG_Payless/Shutterstock.com • 245b Subbotina Anna/Shutterstock.com • 246t GSPhotography/Shutterstock.com • 246c Vlado Radosa/Shutterstock.com • 246br Ortodox/Shutterstock.com • 246bl gavrila bogdan/Shutterstock.com • 247t Ryusuke Komori/Shutterstock.com • 247c matin/Shutterstock.com • 247b Brent Hofacker/Shutterstock.com • 248t P.Kanchana/Shutterstock.com • 248b Razmarinka/Shutterstock.com • 249t phloen/Shutterstock.com • 249c Silatip/Shutterstock.com • 249bl vainillaychile/Shutterstock.com • 249br Aliwak/Shutterstock.com • 250t Izf/Shutterstock.com • 250c nookieme/Shutterstock.com • 250b Tony Magdaraog/Shutterstock.com • 251t Jillian Cain/Shutterstock.com • 251b International Potato Center • 252–253 HLPhoto/Shutterstock.com • 254t, bl NorGal/Shutterstock.com • 254br wEnDy • 255t My Life Graphic/Shutterstock.com • 255c Maša Sinreih in Valentina Vivod • 255b cyclonebill • 256t Kontos • 256b Tobik/Shutterstock.com • 257 Serg Zastavkin/Shutterstock.com • 258t © M.D. Guiry/AlgaeBase • 258b Stephen Lavery/Shutterstock.com • 259t Akuppa John Wigham • 259b marekuliasz/Shutterstock.com • 260t DoublePHOTO studio/Shutterstock.com • 260b Alice Wiegand, (Lyzzy) • 261t Gabriele Kothe-Heinrich • 261b D. Pimborough/Shutterstock.com • 262t © E. & T. Titlyanov/Institute of Marine Biology RAS, Vladivostok, Russia • 262b DryPot • 263t Okinawa Agent, www.okinawab2b.jp • 263b Eric Moody • 264t marekuliasz/Shutterstock.com • 264b hin255/Shutterstock.com • 265t Edward Westmacott/Shutterstock.com • 265tr Alexandra Lande/Shutterstock.com • 265bl Norasit Kaewsai/istock.com • 265br Akuppa John Wigham • 266t Pete Pahham/Shutterstock.com • 266b Marco Schmidt • 267t Zigzag Mountain Art/Shutterstock.com • 267b David Hanlon/Shutterstock.com • 268t H. Krisp • 268b Kristian Peters-Fabelfroh • 269t CSIRO • 269b jreika/Shutterstock.com • 270 sarsmis/Shutterstock.com • 283 holwichaikawee/Shutterstock.com • 311 Jane Rix/Shutterstock.com • 314 rsooll/Shutterstock.com • 316–317 VicushkaI/Shutterstock.com

Moseley Road wishes to thank all photographers whose images appear in this book. We apologize for any omissions or neglect, and will be pleased to make any corrections in future editions.